The Challenge of Industrial Relations

TRADE UNIONS, MANAGEMENT, AND THE PUBLIC INTEREST

The Challenge of
Industrial Relations

TRADE UNIONS, MANAGEMENT,
AND THE PUBLIC INTEREST

SUMNER H. SLICHTER

Lamont University Professor at Harvard

Cornell University Press

*Ithaca, New York * 1947*

Preface

Bᴇᴛᴡᴇᴇɴ 1933 ᴀɴᴅ 1945 ᴜɴɪᴏɴ ᴍᴇᴍʙᴇʀsʜɪᴘ ɪɴ ᴛʜᴇ United States increased fivefold, from about three million to about fifteen million. Unless unions make grievous blunders and lose confidence of the community (by interunion rivalry, for example), this growth will continue. A union membership of over twenty million within the next decade is a strong probability.

The rise of unions constitutes an epoch-making change in the economy — quite comparable to such institutional changes as the rise of the modern credit system or of the corporation. Unions are no longer simply organizations which put workers in a moderately better bargaining position in dealing with employers. They are seats of great power — of the greatest private economic power in the community. Their policies from now on will be a major determinant of the prosperity of the country. If their policies are farsighted, if unions see their stake in the prosperity of the community as a whole, unions will make a major contribution toward building a greater civilization in America. If unions are narrow, uninformed, and shortsighted in their policies, they will be as great a problem for the community as was the parochialism of the towns and small principalities in the later Middle Ages.

The literature of industrial relations has taken little account of the changed status of unions. The literature still treats unions as underdogs and ignores almost completely both the great problems and the great opportunities created by the power of unions.

The aim of these chapters is to lay the foundation for a more realistic approach to the study of trade unions — to focus attention upon the problems created by unions and upon the tremendous contributions which unions can make to national prosperity and industrial democracy. The treatment is brief and the aim has been to define and open issues rather than to reach definitive conclusions. The material in these chapters was presented as six lectures at Cornell University in November, 1946. The lectures have been revised and amplified, but the printed version is essentially the same as the oral one.

My wife has prepared the index and has suggested many improvements in the manuscript.

SUMNER H. SLICHTER

February, 1947

Contents

The Challenge of Industrial Relations

TRADE UNIONS, MANAGEMENT, AND THE PUBLIC INTEREST

Chapter I

The Labor Movement -
Its Rise and Its Present Status

I

THE LAST HUNDRED YEARS HAVE SEEN THE RISE OF A
new kind of community — a community in which nearly all of the gainfully employed are employees. There
have been societies in which nearly all workers have
been slaves or serfs or self-employed persons. Indeed,
until shortly before the middle of the last century,
the United States was mainly a community of self-
employed. Only within the last hundred years, however, have there been communities in which nearly all
workers are employees. Although modern technology
has been converting the country into a community of
employees, it has not been building a proletariat. Scientists, professional workers, supervisors, artists, teachers,
and other white-collar workers have been increasing
from two to thirteen times as fast as the total working
population, while the number of common laborers has
remained about the same for the last thirty years.[1]

---

[1] Between 1870 and 1940, technical engineers increased over 13 times as
fast as the gainfully employed; bookkeepers, cashiers, and accountants,
8 times; artists, sculptors, and art teachers, 5 times; editors and reporters,

Communities of free employees must be expected to develop cultures, institutions, and points of view which are different in many respects from those found in communities of the self-employed. For example, communities of employees must be expected to have distinctive theories concerning what makes the economy work and how production and employment can best be stimulated. Socialism represents an early expression of a distinctive point of view by the community of employees. Socialists propose changes in economic institutions, but today most of them accept the basic political ideas and institutions of liberal Capitalism. They trust individuals to develop their own ideals and to select their own ends, and they believe that civil rights should protect individuals in the opportunity to acquire information, to hear the views of others, and to express their views. Far more radical than Socialism is Communism, another example of a distinctive point of view developed among employees. The economic program of Communism is essentially the same as that of Socialism, but Communism is far more than an economic philosophy. Communism does not trust individuals to develop their own ideals and to select their own ends; it does not protect them with civil rights. It has no use for the democratic philosophy which was developed by Capitalism to defeat the claims of the absolute monarchs and which is accepted by Socialists. Communism would

---

3.75 times; architects, 3.4 times; musicians and teachers of music, 3 times; college professors and other teachers, 3 times; dentists, 2.7 times; clergymen, religious, social, and welfare workers, 1.6 times. Between 1870 and 1940, college graduates have increased 10 times as fast as the gainfully employed.

undo the political revolutions of the seventeenth and eighteenth centuries and would make the government (in this case "the party") the supreme arbiter of values.

Neither Socialism nor Communism has up to now made much progress in the United States. Here the ideas of Capitalism had such vigor that they continued to dominate men's minds long after the community became composed predominantly of employees. For the first two or three generations of the employee community the professional, supervisory, and white-collar employees accepted the economic ideas of the businessmen and property owners. During the last generation, however, these groups have been thinking more and more as employees. The rise of a community of employees has produced a considerable volume of labor legislation, which the employer-dominated community of the nineteenth century would not have tolerated. In the main, however, American workers appear to believe that the most promising way to advance their interests is through negotiation of more favorable labor contracts with employers — contracts which give the workers higher wages and better working conditions. Hence the growth of trade unionism and the development of collective bargaining in all branches of industry are the most distinctive ways in which the change in the nature of the community is expressing itself.

Today the United States has the largest, most powerful, and most aggressive labor movement which the world has ever seen. The 190-odd national unions recently had nearly 15 million members. Today, though the membership is smaller, they include nearly one-third of the 40 million employees outside agriculture and the professions. About 1.4 million members are professional or clerical workers. Two-thirds of the workers in manufacturing are covered by union agreements and about one-third in nonmanufacturing industries outside of agriculture and the professions. In a number of nonmanufacturing industries, such as coal mining, construction, railroading, and trucking, over four-fifths of the employees are under wage agreements. Retailing, wholesaling, and agriculture are the only important areas of employment in which the proportion of organized employees is low. The trade unions are the most powerful economic organizations in the community — in fact, they are the most powerful economic organizations which the community has ever seen. Their policies will be a major influence in determining how much the community produces, how rapidly it adds to its capital, and how the product of industry is divided.

What have been the principal consequences of the rise of trade unions up to now, and what are likely to be their effects in the future? What principles may be expected to guide the behavior of unions? What problems have been created by the rise of unions, and what new problems are they likely to create? What obligations should the community impose on unions, and what rights should it give them? In short, what should be the policy of the community toward them? These are the basic questions which I shall attempt to answer. In the first chapter I shall survey the development of trade unions in the United States, describe the present condition of the trade union movement, and outline briefly some of the problems which trade unions now present. In the following five chapters I shall examine some of the principal effects of trade unions and some of the principal problems which the rise of unions has created.

II

The development of trade unionism in the United States has been slow. As late as 1900 less than one-tenth of the so-called "industrial" wage earners were organized.[2] Even in 1920, after the First World War, fewer than one out of five industrial wage earners were organized. Except during the early decades of the nineteenth century, trade unionism did not encounter the legal obstacles in the United States which hindered its growth in Great Britain and most continental countries. The community, of course, was hostile to unionism, as one would expect a community to be which derived its point of view principally from businessmen and farmers. The rapid growth of population was a major impediment to the rise of unions because it gave workers such excellent opportunities to advance to better jobs. This encouraged men to think in terms of individual careers and discouraged interest in organizations designed to safeguard the interests of any occupational group. Until 1860, population increased by more than one-third every decade; until 1890, by more than one-fourth; until 1910, by more than one-fifth; and until 1930, by one-sixth. Opportunities to rise in

---

[2] By "industrial" wage earners is meant wage earners in manufacturing and mechanical pursuits, mining, transportation, public utilities, and construction.

the economic scale were even greater than the increase in population indicates, because, as I have just pointed out, the managerial and technical professions were growing far faster than the working population.

Three principal periods stand out in the development of the American labor movement:

1. The "grass roots" stage, which lasted until the decade of the eighties.

2. The stage of the dominance of national unions, with reliance upon nonpolitical methods, which lasted from the eighties until the decade of the thirties.

3. The period of government encouragement of trade unions and active government intervention in industrial relations. This began in 1932 and 1933 with the passage of the Norris-LaGuardia Act and the National Industrial Recovery Act, followed closely by the passage of the Wagner Act, the Social Security Act, and the Fair Labor Standards Act.

In the beginning, the trade union movement was necessarily a grass-roots affair. If men were to be organized, they had to organize themselves. No enduring national union was founded until 1852. By 1873 there were about thirty-three national unions in the country, but most of them were feeble and possessed little authority over the locals. Nearly half of them disappeared in the long depression of the seventies. During the grass-roots stage the basic objectives of the labor movement were ill-defined. Likewise, there was uncertainty concerning the kind of organizations and methods which could best represent the interests of workers. For example, the labor organizations were going through the process of deciding whether they could best advance the interests of workers by concentrating upon collective bargaining, by pressing for social and political reforms, or by simultaneously using both methods. They were finding out by the method of trial and error what kind of organization could most effectively command the interest and support of workers in the American environment.

Gradually it became evident that workers were most interested in relying upon bargaining to get themselves better conditions. It also became evident that bargaining was most effectively conducted by local unions, with the guidance and backing of a national union in the occupation or industry, or by a national union itself. The decade of the eighties was the period when the national trade union first came definitely into its own. The troubles of the unions during the depression of the seventies showed that national control needed to be established over many policies, particularly wage policies and strike policies, and that national treasuries needed to be built up for the purpose of backing local unions. During the eighties the number of national unions grew rapidly. Fifty were formed between 1880 and 1890. In the same period fourteen national unions went out of existence, but the total number grew from 26 to 62 — more than doubling in ten years. During the nineties there was an even stronger growth of national unions — an increase of 40, raising the total from 62 to 102.

The rise of national unions meant, of course, that the trade union movement became less and less a spontaneous grass-roots affair. As the nationals gradually grew stronger, the opposition of employers became stiffer and more carefully planned. This made it less practical for men to organize on their own initiative. Thus the opposition of employers to unions helped to promote the dominance of the national union.

The rise of national unions created two basic problems: (1) whether the labor movement should have a central and superior policy-making and co-ordinating agency; and (2) what should be the relationship between the several national unions. Sooner or later these two problems would have arisen anyway, but they were precipitated by the rapid rise of the Knights of Labor during the eighteen-eighties. The Knights of Labor represented the idea of "one big union"—that is, of a highly centralized labor movement. Furthermore, the Knights stood ready to take in disaffected locals, and, in the case of the cigarmakers, the Knights entered into direct competition for the members of the national union. The American Federation of Labor was formed to protect the national unions from losing their independence to the Knights of Labor, and it was based on two principles: (1) the principle of autonomy, that national unions should be subordinate to no strong and centrally guided co-ordinated agency, but should be left free to manage their own affairs; and (2) the principle of exclusive jurisdiction, that there can be only one legitimate union in one recognized field of jurisdiction.

The success of the American Federation of Labor in competition with the Knights of Labor meant that the American labor movement developed on the basis of these two principles, autonomy and exclusive jurisdiction. The personal convictions of dominant leaders, headed by Samuel Gompers, also meant that the trade unions confined themselves pretty narrowly to collective bargaining and sought little help from the government in improving conditions of work. Indeed, the national leaders of the unions regarded proposals for most forms of social legislation with hostility because such arrangements could make the government a competitor of the unions. The growth of national unions and the centralization of policy-making in their hands meant that the control of the labor movement rested largely with professional labor leaders. The jobs of union president, vice president, organizer, or national representative are usually full-time jobs and require specialized ability. Experience increases a man's usefulness. Furthermore, the ordinary work of directing the administration of union affairs enables national officers to build up an organization to keep them in office. Hence, there has been little competition for national office, and the tenure of national union presidents has frequently been rather long.

The ascendency of the professional labor leader has been accentuated by the fact that American unions combine in full-time officers the responsibility both for making policies and for executing policies. In this respect the American practice differs from the British. In the British unions the professional officers are executors of policies and advisers on policy-making, but the principal responsibility for policy-making is in the hands of unpaid executive boards.

For two generations the American labor movement

developed quietly and at a moderate rate on the basis of the three principles of autonomy, exclusive jurisdiction, and reliance upon collective bargaining rather than upon labor legislation to improve the condition of workers. Trade unions did support workmen's compensation laws, but in the main these three principles were accepted. Efforts to interest the trade unions in labor legislation early in the nineties and at the end of the First World War proved abortive. The complete acceptance of the above-mentioned three principles and the unchallenged leadership of the professional labor leaders made the period 1886 to 1933 one of stability. Paradoxically, the strong opposition of employers helped to keep the labor movement stable. It strengthened the position of the officers by making it difficult to organize workers. This protected the officers of unions from the competition of new leaders. In particular, the opposition of employers helped make the principle of exclusive jurisdiction work by discouraging competition between national unions for members and by preventing independent movements to organize workers from making much headway. Only organization drives backed by the national unions had much chance of success.

The period of stability was terminated by the Great Depression of 1929, which broke the influence of business upon the thinking of the community and led the government to embark upon the policy of actively encouraging workers to organize and of regulating the working conditions in nearly all plants engaged in interstate commerce. A preliminary step in the government's encouragement of trade union organizations was the passage of the Norris-LaGuardia Act in 1932. It was quickly followed by the National Industrial Recovery Act in 1933 and the Wagner Act in 1935. The principal manifestations of the regulation of working conditions by the national government were the Social Security Act and the Fair Labor Standards Act — the first passed in 1935, the second in 1938. Underlying these changes in national policy was a constitutional revolution. The Supreme Court suddenly abandoned long-held views concerning both the scope of the national government's authority over interstate commerce and the extent to which private rights may be restricted in order to permit Congress to carry out its ideas of promoting community interests.

Helped by friendly government policies, trade unions rapidly spread their membership outside the ranks of skilled craftsmen, to which it had mainly been confined prior to 1933. The first large new groups to come into the labor movement were the semiskilled factory workers. Organization soon began to grow rapidly, however, among retail clerks, white-collar workers, and supervisors, who had traditionally regarded themselves as "above" trade unionism.

The changes in public policy brought about by the Great Depression did much more than produce a spectacular spurt in union membership. They forced changes in the basic principles on which the labor movement had been operating. The principle of autonomy (that each union should be free to manage its own affairs) has survived the changes in public policy, at least thus far. The principle of exclusive jurisdiction and the principle of relying almost entirely upon collective bargaining rather than upon labor legislation both broke down.

The principle of exclusive jurisdiction broke down for two reasons. One was that government protection of the workers' right to organize stimulated grass-roots organization of workers. The scope of many of the new unions did not correspond to the jurisdictional lines recognized by the American Federation of Labor, which was made up predominantly of craft unions. The new local unions frequently resisted being broken up in order to fit into the official pattern. The second reason for the breakdown of the principle of exclusive jurisdiction was that the government's encouragement of organization made many union leaders eager to take full advantage of the opportunity to expand membership. Some men inside the American Federation of Labor wished to form unions along industrial lines when that seemed to be the preference of the workers. Most of the leaders of the craft unions were unwilling to relinquish their jurisdictional claims. The result was the split in the labor movement and the ultimate formation of the Congress of Industrial Organizations. The C.I.O. is a symbol of how completely the principle of exclusive jurisdiction has broken down.

The breakdown of the principle of exclusive jurisdiction means that there has been anarchy in the labor movement, with competition for members becoming more widespread and more unrestrained. More and more unions have not hesitated to employ strikes or boycotts to force men to change their allegiance. The A. F. of L. building trades' workers seek to control the allegiance of the makers of building materials by refusing to handle materials produced by C.I.O. workers. The teamsters' union uses control over deliveries to force workers in warehouses to leave other unions and join the teamsters' union. In some communities the teamsters have used their control over deliveries to force all brewery workers into the teamsters' union. The C.I.O. longshoremen use their control of the waterfront to control the allegiance of men on vessels and men in warehouses. When a union is dominated by a powerful individual, his prestige depends partly upon the success of the union in increasing its membership in competition with other unions. Consequently, the competition between unions becomes competition between ambitious union leaders for power, influence, and prestige. As the competition for members has gone on and as rivalries have become keener, unions have shown less and less respect for the well-established jurisdictions of other unions belonging to the same federation.

The principle of relying almost solely upon collective bargaining to improve the working conditions of employees broke down, partly because the depression brought great problems with which collective bargaining could not deal, and partly because the rapid expansion of union membership brought into the trade union movement new leaders and new members who did not accept the traditional reliance upon collective bargaining. Collective bargaining, for example, could not provide the workers with adequate protection against loss of income from unemployment. The leaders of the American Federation of Labor refused at the conventions of the Federation in 1930 and in 1931 to demand unemployment insurance. Indeed, as late as July, 1932, the *Weekly News Letter* of the A. F. of L. contained a strong denunciation of unemployment insurance. In the fall of 1932, however, the convention demanded unemployment compensation. When the Roosevelt Administration proposed a comprehensive Social Security Act and later a Fair Labor Standards Act, the leaders of the trade unions abandoned their traditional positions and supported this legislation.

III

What is the present state of the trade union movement in the United States? Six principal characteristics of the trade union movement stand out:

1. Unions have tremendous power. No longer do they cover a small fraction of the work force. About seven million jobs in American industry may be held only by men who are union members or whom unions are willing to accept as members. About eleven million employees who work in union shops or closed shops or under maintenance-of-membership clauses hold their jobs only so long as they keep in good standing in their unions. No longer are most unions underdogs. The strongest unions, as I have pointed out, are the most powerful economic organizations which the country has ever seen. One cannot conceive of the railroads, even if

they were not bound by law to render continuous service, daring to cut off the country from railroad service. Steel producers would not dare combine for the purpose of depriving the country of steel; no combination of coal operators would dare cut off the supply of coal. Yet in each of these industries during the last year unions have not hesitated to stop production in order to enforce their demands — in some cases, very trivial demands.

2. The leadership of the trade union movement is pretty largely in the hands of full-time professional officers of national unions. Many of these men are almost as remote from the rank and file members of the union as are the heads of large corporations from their employees. Very much the same problems of keeping in touch with the rank and file and of communicating with the rank and file confront the officers of national unions as confront the officers of large corporations. Most of the important decisions of unions are made by national officers or their appointed representatives. The "town meeting" ideal of trade unionism, which envisages widespread participation from the rank and file in making decisions of policy, gets farther from realization every day.

3. The rise of professional labor leaders has led a number of unions to be dominated by individuals or small groups of individuals. Their government is best described as "dictatorship" or oligarchy. This does not mean that the union heads force their will upon unwilling members. On the contrary, the men who operate personal governments are careful to keep them-

selves popular and to pursue policies which arouse the approval of the rank and file. The rank and file, however, have little to say in selecting the policies. Furthermore, in these unions any competition for office at the national level is ruthlessly suppressed.

4. There is strong rivalry between unions. This rivalry goes far beyond the two groups of unions which are organized, respectively, into the American Federation of Labor and the Congress of Industrial Organizations. It extends to unions within each of the federations, and in some cases it takes the form of personal rivalries between men at the head of unions. These rivalries, rather than economic considerations, have played in recent years an increasingly important role in determining union policies. The rapid growth of union membership has stimulated interunion competition because it has brought into the labor movement millions of men who have no strong allegiance to a particular union and who are quite ready to join another union if the second one seems more aggressive and more powerful than the first. Even the members of old and well-established unions are often ready to switch to unions which they regard as more aggressive and tougher than their own union.

5. The trade union movement is characterized by strong particularism and by lack of an organization which represents labor as a whole. Despite the fact that a majority of nonsupervisory and nontechnical employees in American industry are now organized, labor *as a whole* is still unorganized. The 190-odd national unions represent that many different groups of work-

ers. Each union, quite naturally, is concerned with the conditions of its own members rather than with the conditions of labor as a whole. As Hoxie has well said, "The viewpoint of unionism is primarily a group viewpoint."[3] No organization with authority or prestige represents labor as a whole or concerns itself with whether the policies of particular unions are injuring labor as a whole. The top policy-makers of the two federations are also the heads of powerful unions and are more interested in running their own unions as they see fit than in developing policies which advance the interests of labor as a whole or which restrain individual unions from injuring the rest of labor.

6. The trade union movement has not yet adjusted itself to the increasingly important role which the government is playing in determining conditions of employment. The regulation of many conditions of work by legislation gives workers a much greater stake in public policy than they have ever had before. It creates new problems for the unions, partly because the regulation of working conditions by the government limits the importance of unions, and partly because unions are designed to be bargaining organizations rather than political organizations and are hence not well adapted to operating in the political field. In order to be effective bargaining organizations, unions need to open their doors to all persons in an occupation or industry regardless of whether these persons are Democrats, Republicans, or Socialists. Although the labor movement has virtually committed itself to substantial reliance

---

[3] R. F. Hoxie, *Trade Unionism in the United States*, p. 282.

upon legislation as well as upon collective bargaining to improve working conditions, it has not yet worked out an accepted policy for political operations. Some leaders wish to operate as a pressure group through both political parties; some wish to seize control of the party machinery of one or both of the major parties; some wish to build up an independent labor party.

IV

What problems emerge from the rise of the labor movement? Six principal groups of problems have been created by the rise of unions:

1. The effect of unions upon the management of business enterprises.

2. The economic consequences of the wage policies of unions.

3. The effect of unions upon the rights and duties of their members within unions — their opportunity to participate in the making of policy decisions within the union and their rights with respect to the imposition of discipline by the union.

4. The effectiveness of collective bargaining in producing settlements of industrial disputes.

5. The effect of the enormous power of unions upon the interests of the community as a whole.

6. The effect of unions upon the political life of the community.

The last of these questions I shall not undertake to discuss. The following chapters, however, will each deal with one of the other five problems. Let us notice briefly the nature of each of them.

1. How does the rise of trade unions affect the management of business concerns? It means the introduction of a separate organization, with its own purposes,

policies, and leaders, into nearly every plant — an organization which puts the personal interests of workers ahead of production just as the managerial organization puts production ahead of many of the personal interests of the workers. Three basic questions arise:

a. Will collective bargaining create shop rules which are favorable to the production of the largest national output?

b. Will the existence of organizations authorized to challenge the decisions of management make for more efficient administration of business enterprises?

c. Can two organizations with different objectives work together in harmony?

Employers, in dealing with unions, may be regarded as the bargaining representatives of consumers; unions bargain for employees, who are producers. When employees are unorganized, the interests of workers are likely to receive too little consideration to make possible the largest net national product. Is the more adequate representation of producer interests brought about by trade unions favorable to the creation of the largest possible net product? The procedure of leaving the rights and duties of management and the rights and duties of workers to be determined by bargaining power seems somewhat primitive. Why should bargaining power be so balanced as to yield the distribution of rights and duties which makes possible the largest net product? Has it been possible to give management conditions which are favorable for production only by refusing to concede demands which the workers regard as important? Has fairly complete concession of demands which the workers regard as important substantially impeded production?

The agreements between management and unions give unions the right to challenge many decisions of management and to compel management to justify its decisions. Does this make managements more alert? Does it make for more carefully considered decisions and for better managerial practice? Or does the right of the union to challenge decisions of company officials hamstring management and limit managerial efficiency?

The management and the union in a plant may find it easy or difficult to get on together. Their objectives and policies need to be adjusted to each other. The problem may be compared to one of adjusting relations between two countries. If management and the union are successful in adjusting their different objectives and policies, there will be harmony in the plant. If they are unsuccessful, there will be discord. Obviously the efficiency of production will depend upon whether there is harmony or discord.

2. What are the economic consequences of the wage policies of trade unions? Many wage earners have unquestioned faith in the possibilities of raising the income of labor by bargaining for higher wages. In particular, they have great faith in the possibility of raising the income of labor at the expense of profits. Is this faith of wage earners in bargaining power justified? Can the price of labor relative to commodity prices be raised by bargaining power? If so, will payrolls be increased or diminished? Will labor's share in the national income be raised or lowered?

Collective bargaining is bound to affect both the structure of wages and the behavior of wages. One may expect the structure of wages under collective bargaining to reflect, not the skill and responsibility required of workers in different occupations and industries or the relative supply of labor and the demand for it, but, on the one hand, the differing bargaining power of the 50,000 local unions or of the 190-odd national unions and, on the other hand, the bargaining power of the employer or the employers' association. The wage structure resulting from collective bargaining will bring about a different distribution of labor between occupations, industries, and places from that produced by free markets. Hence, industry under collective bargaining will not produce goods in the same proportions as under free markets.

May the upward pressure of unions on wages be expected to raise the rate of technological change? Is collective bargaining likely to push up the price of labor faster than engineers and managers are able to raise output per man-hour? If it does, can increases in prices be counted upon to offset the difference or must collective bargaining be expected to produce chronic and substantial unemployment? If collective bargaining produces chronic unemployment, is there anything which can be done about it?

3. How do trade unions conduct their own affairs? Are their procedures democratic? Are the rights and freedoms of their members safeguarded and respected? These are questions of great importance because trade unions are governments which impose many rules and duties on men and which act for men on important matters. About eleven million workers in American in-

dustry who work in union shops, in closed shops, or under maintenance-of-membership clauses hold their jobs only so long as they are in good standing in their unions. If trade unions are not democratic, an important area of decision-making is not encompassed by democratic processes.

Whether or not trade unions in practice are democratic is one thing. Even more important is the question whether trade unions should be *expected* to be democratic. Do they act under the conditions and in the kinds of situations that are favorable to democracy? Trade unions ordinarily lack certain institutions which are regarded as important to the success of democracy in the body politic. For example, trade unions do not ordinarily have a free press or an independent judiciary. The administration controls the union's journal, and it usually appoints trial boards which administer union discipline — or controls their appointment. Political parties, an essential part of the apparatus of democracy in the body politic, do not work well in unions, and usually do not exist. A trade union may be compared to a national government which is engaged in the main in conducting foreign relations. Unions, in order to be cohesive and to deal effectively with employers, must build up unity among their members and must convince employers that the union members are solidly behind the union policies and the union leaders. In other words, while the community can afford processes in the body politic which emphasize differences, at least in domestic matters, unions must emphasize agreement. Criticizing the administration or finding fault with policies may easily become serious offenses in unions, causing a man's loyalty to be brought into question and possibly causing him to be tried for "creating dissension" or "conduct unbecoming to a union member."

The strong and aggressive men who win their way to the top in unions are not likely to sit back and let the rank and file argue over what program the union should adopt. The strong leader takes the initiative by proposing a program and inviting the rank and file to support it. It is not the only program which the leader might have proposed, and it may not be as popular as would have been some other program which the leader did not happen to think of. Nevertheless, it is usually popular, and the union members ordinarily understand the importance of getting strongly behind the official program rather than debating possible alternatives.

It is plain that the standards which one is accustomed to apply in appraising the political life of the community at large do not necessarily apply to trade unions. After one has discovered what the realities of union political life are and what conditions produce these realities, one must construct the standards which one intends to apply, and then one must decide how realization of these standards may be promoted.

4. What can be done to make collective bargaining produce agreements in a higher proportion of cases, to make the process of bargaining take into account more completely the problems and needs of union members and of employers, and to make the settlements more adequately reflect these needs? Experience indicates

that in prewar years four out of five agreements, and possibly a much higher proportion, were renewed without strike or lockout. Nevertheless, in only six out of the last thirty years have there been less than 1,000 industrial disputes, and in only thirteen have there been less than 2,000.

The actual practice of collective bargaining falls far short of the theoretical ideal. In theory men enter bargaining conferences with open minds, ready to persuade and be persuaded. In the course of negotiations, each side in theory is expected to learn more about the problems of the other and to gain new ideas concerning what would be a fair bargain. In practice, each side often begins negotiations with a firm resolution to stand by its position and not to be influenced by any facts or arguments which the other side may advance. Often the two sides make public their positions so that compromise is difficult. Being tough, unreasonable, and inflexible is sometimes adopted as a definite technique of negotiation — as a way of forcing the other side to make concessions. Too often it works.

Collective bargaining cannot be a satisfactory procedure for adjusting wages if the results of bargaining depend primarily upon the bargaining power of the two sides. Collective bargaining must be an appeal to facts and to reason, not an appeal to mere strength. This means that criteria must be developed which express the community's interest in the structure of wages and in the movement of wages. It also means that ways and means must be developed by which bargaining shall be based upon these criteria. What can be done by unions, employers, and the community to improve the practice of collective bargaining? What can be done to make collective bargaining an appeal to reason rather than an appeal to force?

A frequent suggestion is that the Conciliation Service be developed into a more effective aid for collective bargaining. No one will dispute this suggestion. Nevertheless, the role of conciliation and its limitations should be plainly understood. Too much conciliation, a too-ready disposition on the part of the Conciliation Service to intervene, may impede the development of responsible collective bargaining. The expectation that the conciliators will intervene may lead each side to stick to extreme positions, counting upon the conciliators to save their faces by begging them to make concessions in the public interest. Hence, the proper role of the Conciliation Service needs to be carefully explored.

5. What does the community propose to do to control the enormous power of unions and to realize the great constructive potentialities of unions? The policy of encouraging the growth of unions has succeeded beyond the fondest hopes of its supporters. Unions are larger, more powerful, and more aggressive than anyone ever dreamed they would be. When the public undertook to encourage unions, it thought that it was helping downtrodden and oppressed men to help themselves. It did not foresee the great power that it was placing in the hands of a few men.

Now that this great power has been created, the community must decide what to do about it. The great power of unions has manifested itself in several ways — in the imposition of conditions on employers which reduce the productivity of industry and thus reduce the standard of living of the community, in the refusal of a few unions to engage in bargaining on important issues, in the use of strikes to compel or attempt to compel violations of law, in the use of strikes or threats of strike to force changes in public policy and to coerce the government, and, finally, in the calling of strikes which deprive the public of essential services.

These questions, it will be observed, raise the basic and highly controversial issue of restricting the right to strike. Many labor leaders and others believe that restrictions on the right to strike are incompatible with free labor and even with democratic institutions. Would these upholders of the right to strike contend that workers should have the right to strike to compel employers to violate the law — the Wagner Act, for example? Would they contend that prohibiting wage earners from striking to compel changes in public policy undermines democratic institutions? Should men have the right to strike or to engage in boycotts to make warfare against other unions — to compel workers to change their union affiliation? Should the United Automobile Workers, for example, be permitted to decide that they will handle only automobile parts made by other C.I.O. workmen? Are there any occupations or industries in which the duties of the workers or the need of the public for continuous service make it inappropriate to give the workers the right to strike? Should the right to strike be given nurses, attendants, or guards in hospitals, in institutions for the insane or handicapped, and in prisons; to employees in the electric light and power industry? It is plain that conventional thinking about the right to strike is obsolete. The community must face squarely the question as to whether strikes for certain purposes should be made illegal and whether strikes in certain essential occupations or industries should be made illegal.

Finally, and most important of all, is the question of how trade unions affect the scales of value of the community and the relative importance attached by people to their special interests and to their common interests. Two possibilities exist. The rise of labor organizations may tend to make people narrow and parochial and to weaken their interest in community-wide problems. Or trade unions may turn out to be extremely useful agencies of communication through which bricklayers, plumbers, automobile workers, and others become more completely aware of their stake in the prosperity of the community as a whole and in the effects of policies of particular unions upon the general welfare. What conditions will determine which kind of organization unions turn out to be? What can be done to make unions more effective instruments for advancing the general welfare?

V

So rapid has been the rise of organized labor and so recent its acquisition of great power that the community is unaware both of the many difficult problems which trade unions have created and of the tremendous contribution which trade unions are capable of making toward building a greater civilization. Indeed, the community has not had time to become well aware of the new facts of life and to see what new problems and new opportunities have emerged. Much less has it had time to adjust its duties and emotions to the new facts. The public is bewildered and surprised. Time will obviously be required for the public to learn the new facts and to reach decisions about policies. The public may have to continue to learn the hard way by experiencing costly interruptions to service while unions strike to compel violations of law, to coerce the government, to deprive other workers of the right to join unions of their own choice, or to interrupt essential services. The purpose of this volume is to reduce the necessity of learning by experience — to make possible in some small measure the substitution of forethought for experience — and to give to trade union members and to the man-in-the-street a clearer vision of the constructive possibilities of trade unions.

Chapter II

The Effect of Trade Unions on the

Management of Business Enterprises

I

THE ESTABLISHMENT OF A TRADE UNION IN A PLANT produces a revolution in the problems of management. It means that operations are conducted within the framework of rules which management can change only by negotiation with the union. It means that the decisions of management may be challenged by representatives of the employees. It means that the employees who had to obey or be fired have become a society of free men with the equivalent of civil rights and with opportunity to challenge decisions of management. Furthermore, it means the introduction of an organization which has its own objectives, policies, and leaders. The objectives and policies of the union differ from those of management and may conflict with management's objectives and policies.

The existence of two organizations (the management organization and the union) and of two sets of leaders (officers of management and officers of the union) has tremendous possibilities for either harmony or discord. As I pointed out in the first chapter, there are three basic questions which should be considered:

1. Will the shop rules produced by collective bargaining increase or reduce the net national product?

2. Will the presence of the union make for better administrative practices?

3. Can the management and the union, despite their different objectives, live in harmony? Or will organized rivalry between them impede the efficiency of operations?

II

The introduction of collective bargaining into plants raises in an acute form the question of how far enterprises should be run in the interests of consumers and how far in the interests of employees and of the union as an organization. The consumers' interest is in methods of production which make possible low money costs; the employees' interest is in security, in a comfortable pace of work, and in the avoidance of too much competition among workers. In addition, the union as an organization may be interested in encouraging certain methods of operation which promote cohesiveness among the workers and strengthen the solidarity of the union and in keeping out methods of operation which have the opposite effects.

In this bargaining, management, of course, represents the interests of consumers. This fact is frequently overlooked, but it is of great importance. The lower the costs of production, the lower competition forces prices or the higher it forces quality. Hence, in bargaining for lower costs managements are representing consumers. This is true even though competition be "monopolistic."[1] The fact that competition is monopolistic does not mean that it is not keen. It simply means that sufficient real or imaginary differences exist between the products or services rendered by rival sellers so that competition relates to quality and service as well as to price. When most of an industry is in the hands of a few large sellers who take account of the effect of price cuts upon the prices of their competitors (oligopoly), there may be some delay in the passing on of savings of costs to consumers. There are limits, however, to this delay. One reason is that the sales of many products can be greatly expanded by reductions in price. Hence, even when the price cut by one large seller is promptly met by other large sellers, all sellers may gain an advantageous increase in sales. Another reason is that only rarely is an industry *entirely* in the hands of a few large firms. There are usually small enterprises which find it advantageous to convert reductions in cost promptly into reductions in price and to expand at the expense of their larger rivals.[2]

---

[1] The term "monopolistic" competition, though a good one for economists, carries misleading connotations for the layman, and has even introduced some confusion into the thinking of economists. The impression has gained currency that "monopolistic" competition is somehow less competitive than "pure" competition. As a matter of fact, monopolistic competition is a *higher* form of competition than the so-called "pure" competition. It means that competition relates *both* to quality and to price. Obviously it is an advantage to have competition with respect to quality as well as to price. Confusion has arisen because oligopoly is frequently associated with monopolistic competition. Oligopoly may retard the transmission of technological progress to consumers. It is oligopoly, not monopolistic competition, which is undesirable.

[2] The concerns which are commonly regarded as the price "leaders" in various industries are often price "followers" rather than leaders. The real

Achieving the largest net national product requires that a balance be struck between the interests of consumers and the interests of workers. Management must not be permitted to go too far in imposing high human costs on workers in order to get more output of commodities, and workers must not be permitted to go too far in impeding the output of commodities in order to get low human costs. Achieving the largest net national product, however, requires more than a proper balancing of the interests of consumers and the interests of workers under any particular set of economic institutions. It also requires that of the several sets of economic institutions under which goods might be made, such as free markets or collective bargaining, the institutions be selected which yield the largest product in relation to human costs.

Unfortunately, there is no way by which the relative productivity of labor and capital under individual bargaining and under collective bargaining can be compared. It is plain, however, that arrangements which exist under individual bargaining may fall short of yielding the largest possible net product. For example, competition between workers may push the speed of work so high that men are worn out at such an early

---

leadership comes from small enterprises.

Indirect evidence of the transmission of savings in costs to consumers is furnished by the long-time downward drift in the ratio of corporate profits to the national income despite the fact that a steadily growing fraction of the national output is produced by corporations. During the five years, 1909–1913, corporate profits were 7.4 per cent of the national income; in the three years, 1937, 1939, and 1940, corporate profits were 6.4 per cent of the national income. Even in the war years, 1943 to 1945, corporate profits were only 6.1 per cent of the national income.

age that their lifetime output is less than it would be at a slower pace. Or the absence of jointly determined rules may prevent the introduction of arrangements, such as seniority rules and the right of workers to have discharges reviewed, which substantially reduce the human costs of production without materially reducing the output of commodities.

No assurance exists, of course, that collective bargaining will produce better compromises than individual bargaining between the interests of consumers and the interests of workers. Collective bargaining, for example, may introduce arrangements which substantially limit output without greatly reducing the human costs of production. It seems clear, however, that in most shops collective bargaining has brought about a better compromise between the interests of consumers and the interests of workers. It is not possible to prove this conclusion by measurements, but it is possible to give many examples of changes in rules and policies which greatly improve conditions for workers without substantially raising the money costs of production or without raising them at all. In a few cases, changes brought about by unions have reduced money costs of production. The following are illustrations of changes in rules and policies which do not seriously raise money costs but which substantially improve conditions of work for employees:

1. The requirement that all discharges must be for a good cause and subject to review. This probably is the most important single accomplishment of trade unions.

2. The requirement that drops in the demand for labor shall

be met either by equal division of work or layoffs in accordance with seniority. Although nonunion shops have gradually shown a tendency to pay more attention to length of service in making layoffs, there has been no certainty that individual cases would be decided on this basis. Hence, no one was just sure where he stood. The introduction of certainty has been a great step forward.

3. The requirement that employees displaced by technological change shall be given the first opportunity to learn jobs under the new technique and shall be trained at company expense while learning.

4. The protection of older workers against discrimination by requiring that they be given preference on certain types of work or that a certain proportion of men above a given age be hired for each job.

5. The reform of pension plans so that a man who resigns from an employer's service does not lose the pension rights which he accumulated.

6. Rationalization of wage structures within plants bringing rates more nearly in line with the skill and responsibilities of different jobs. Much rationalization of wage structure has occurred without demands from unions, and in some union plants little or nothing has been done because the union officers feared that wage changes which gave more to some members than to others would arouse dissatisfaction among the rank and file. The wage structures which developed during the days when management's power was unchallenged are full of inconsistencies and anomalies. The wage structure in most plants has grown in a hit-or-miss fashion and is grievously in need of reform. Pressure from the unions has produced many reforms.

Not only have many rules introduced into shops by collective bargaining increased the net national product, but bargaining has produced indirect results which have been good for the community. For example, protection of workers against arbitrary discharge and their right to challenge the decision of management gives employees a better chance to be independent and self-respecting and to live the lives of normal human beings while in the shop. Hence, under trade unions a different type of man grows up in industry. Furthermore, the protection given to workers against arbitrary discharge and the requirement that decreases in the demand for labor be met either by equal division of work or by lay-offs in accordance with seniority have converted millions of jobs which previously had been held on a day-to-day basis into lasting connections which cannot arbitrarily be broken off by the employer. Seniority rules, it is true, are of only limited help to men at the bottom of the seniority list. Men in the upper half of the list and very often the men in the higher two-thirds are reasonably certain of steady work. Even the men at the bottom of the list have the advantage of knowing definitely where they stand. Furthermore, the seniority rules in many agreements give men who are laid off the right to be rehired. This conversion of millions of jobs into more or less reliable sources of income is an economic fact of great importance because it gives millions of workers for the first time in their lives a reasonable opportunity to make long-range plans. It ought to contribute significantly to the stability of the economy.

III

Although the rise of collective bargaining has quite generally improved the balance between the interests of consumers and the interests of employees, unions have imposed some conditions in industry which give relatively little benefit to employees but which impose considerable impediments upon efficiency and, therefore, upon production. Examples of such rules are:

1. The requirement that men be hired through the union office or through a union hiring hall. It is part of the management's skill to determine who is best fitted for a given job. Consequently, the rule that management take men in the order sent by a union prevents management from exercising an important part of its skill. This is true even though the management has the right to reject men sent by the union. This privilege simply enables management to reject the worst men, not to pick the best ones. In order to prevent the union business agent from showing favoritism, unions which require hiring through union hiring halls usually provide that men shall be sent to jobs according to the length of time they have been out of work, subject to the qualification that they are fitted by training or experience for the job. This may be a good way of equalizing the burden of unemployment, but it is not a good way of getting the men assigned to the jobs for which they are best qualified. Furthermore, it is difficult to prevent favoritism. Hence, union hiring halls easily become devices for keeping the "ins" in office. For example, if a job is likely to be a short one, union members may be reluctant to be sent to it because they will lose their position on the hiring list. Favoritism may be shown by holding that the man is not qualified for the job and need not be sent to it, thereby forcing someone else to take the short-term job.

2. The requirement that promotions be made in accordance with strict seniority. This rule is far more common than the compulsory use of union hiring halls. Although layoffs may well be based upon strict seniority, promotions need to be based upon merit. Otherwise merit is of no use in helping a man get ahead, and an important incentive for efficiency is destroyed. The great majority of workers in a plant may well be opposed to promotion on the basis of merit, because this principle helps the superior few at the expense of the mediocre many.[3] Rules requiring that promotion be on the basis of straight seniority do much to rob many thousands of jobs of their future. Each member of the community in his capacity of consumer has a strong interest that promotions be by merit. Furthermore, every consumer has an interest that industry be kept dynamic and creative by keeping the door of opportunity open to superior ability wherever it may be found.

The determination of merit is a responsibility of management. Merit will obviously differ in various situations. An important aspect of merit is a man's adaptability to the people with whom he must work. Will he be a good member of a team? Will he add the

---

[3] A recent study of the re-employment of veterans by Robert C. Goodwin, director of the U. S. Employment Service, and Perry Faulkner, chief of Veterans' Employment Service, says: "One of the most pronounced characteristics of the average veteran seeking employment is his natural desire to get a job where he has a chance to advance. These men are anxious to obtain jobs with a future" (Boston *Herald*, December 29, 1946, p. 12). The requirement that promotion be by straight seniority prevents many positions from holding out much opportunity for advancement to superior workers.

proper qualities to the team? Will he improve the balance of the team? Managers are in the best position to answer these questions. Indeed, that is what they are hired for. The requirement that promotions be based on seniority deprives managers of the opportunity to exercise some of their most important skills.

Incidentally, disputes over whether A or B is the better man for a job do not present the kind of question which should be referred to arbitration. That would merely be asking a neutral, who is not necessarily skilled as a manager and who cannot begin to master the facts in the case, to substitute his judgment for that of management — in other words, to replace the judgment of a professional with the judgment of an amateur. An appropriate question for arbitration, however, would be the charge that management did not exercise its discretion in good faith, that it was actuated by ulterior motives.

3. Make-work rules. These are an expensive arrangement because they impose a lasting burden in order to give temporary relief. This fact is usually overlooked. Make-work rules are ordinarily imposed in order to take up slack in employment. Rarely are more than a few months required for the labor force in an industry to adjust itself to a drop in demand. All that the workers can hope to get out of the make-work rule is some relief during the period which otherwise would be required for the labor supply to adjust itself to the demand. For this small gain they impose a lasting burden on the community. It is poetic justice, perhaps, that a large part of the burden falls upon the workers who impose

it. The capacity of unions to impose higher costs upon employers, of course, is limited. Hence if a union elects to impose higher costs in the form of make-work rules, it is less able to impose higher costs in the form of higher wages.

4. The requirement that the consent of the union be given before certain rates are put into effect, jobs reclassified, standards changed, or working conditions changed, or that certain arrangements, such as job evaluation plans, be jointly worked out between the union and the employer. Some unions believe that such an arrangement would be highly advantageous to the workers.

If the employer is hostile to the union and the union is not protected by the union shop, the closed shop, or a maintenance-of-membership clause, the union may need to require that rates, standards, and other working conditions be jointly determined to prevent the employer from discriminating against union members. Joint determination of rates, standards, and working conditions may enable the union to pursue a policy of obstruction by refusing to consent to new rates and new conditions. In this way the union may be able to force the employer to make a variety of concessions. Such a tactic on the part of the union, however, is pretty certain to create bad relations with the employer. Furthermore, a policy of obstruction stirs up a demand from this, that, and the other small group of members that the union use its power to get special privileges for the group. Such privileges add to the employer's costs in ways which are of no general benefit to the union members and which, in fact, limit the ability of the union to obtain general concessions.

Under normal conditions the requirement that the management bargain with the union *before* making changes in rates, job classifications, standards, and other working conditions has disadvantages both for the union and for the management. Among the principal disadvantages are:

1. Such a requirement prevents management from promptly putting changes into effect. In many industries, particularly seasonal ones, this deprives employers of business and the workers of earnings. Management should have the right and the opportunity to act promptly and in some cases on the basis of a hunch and should not as a regular routine be required to explain its ideas and persuade the union representatives that its ideas are correct.

2. The requirement compels the union to maintain a large and expensive staff of experts — time-study men and standards men. Since the number of cases in which there is serious disagreement over rates or standards is a small fraction of the total, this expense is almost completely a waste of money, especially since the union has a chance to get rates or standards changed through the regular grievance procedure.

3. The requirement compels the union to take a position on changes before they have been tried out and before the union is in a good position to know whether it favors or opposes a given change.

4. The requirement creates the danger that the union's technicians will approve changes which the rank and file may later regard as objectionable. Thus a rift, leading to lack of confidence, may grow up between the rank and file and the union representatives. An extreme case of this sort occurred in the Naumkeag Steam Spinning Company, where the rank and

file eventually formed a new union of their own.[4] It is better for the solidarity of the union that the management take full responsibility for changes, leaving the union free to criticize and challenge them in case it sees fit.

Unions should, of course, have the right to challenge such changes after they have been made, through the regular grievance machinery. It may be wise for management to submit new rates, changes in job classification, or other changes in conditions to the union for advice and criticism before making them. Valuable suggestions which prevent later grievances may in this way be obtained.

Sometimes an attempt is made to stretch the terms of an agreement into requiring that no changes may be made in working conditions without bargaining with the union. A more or less standard recognition clause in the agreement between the Postal Telegraph Company and the American Communications Association was held by one arbitrator to require that the company bargain with the union over every change in working conditions. This interpretation would virtually have given the union an opportunity to conduct a strike without calling any worker off the job. The union could have blocked any change in working conditions to which it objected by the simple expedient of challenging every change until the company withdrew the objectionable one. The arbitrator's decision was reversed in another case by a second arbitrator.

---

[4] The Naumkeag case is discussed in my book, *Union Policies and Industrial Management*, pp. 532–559.

IV

Collective bargaining has had important effects upon administrative practices in many plants. Usually these effects have been favorable to production, but in some cases they have not.

One of the most important ways in which collective bargaining has improved administration has been through the establishment of grievance machinery through which workers are able to challenge the decisions of management. Under most agreements the right of workers to challenge the decisions of management is very broad, not being limited to cases in which the worker charges that management has violated the agreement, but including any case in which the worker charges management with doing something unfair or unreasonable. For example, a study of 200 agreements shows that only violations of the agreement are defined as grievances in forty-five cases; only violations of the agreement or disciplinary action or discharge in nine cases; and in 139 cases a grievance may be *any* action (or failure to act) which the worker charges is unfair or unjust. In seven cases no definition of a grievance is given.

The right of workers to challenge decisions of management has led supervisors to make decisions more carefully and to have the facts in hand before reaching a conclusion. The setting of piece rates and standards of production is an illustration. With the union able to challenge any rate or standard, management must be prepared to show who was timed, under what conditions, and for how long. The right of workers to challenge decisions of management has led many concerns to develop policies to replace snap judgments and off-the-cuff decisions on many points. Some companies have issued labor-relations manuals for their supervisors. In part, these manuals are intended to help supervisors comply with the terms of agreement between the company and the unions or to comply with laws such as the Wage-Hour Law. In large part, however, they are designed to guide supervisors in handling problems about which management is entitled to exercise its discretion.

A second way in which collective bargaining has improved administration has been by forcing managements to develop better arrangements for consultation between different levels of supervision. For example, in order to avoid confusion from foremen in different departments handling the same problem in different ways, managements have had to develop the practice of having foremen consult with their superiors or with the industrial relations department before making certain types of decision.

A third way in which collective bargaining has improved administration is by bringing about better communication between workers and management. More information for management about the point of view and problems of workers is a by-product of the grievances which workers raise. Grievances, however, are not the only way in which unions bring information to management. The shop stewards and union committees are sources of information because stewards and committeemen are often willing to speak out as the individual worker will not — especially when there is no union in the plant. In some plants collective bargaining has led to the institution of labor-management committees which discuss shop conditions in general.

In a few concerns collective bargaining has also meant better communication downward as well as upward. Some managements, for example, have sought through union representatives to keep the rank and file informed about the business, its plans, its prospects, and its problems. The Baltimore and Ohio Railroad and the Canadian National Railway are examples. A manufacturer in the Middle West insists upon the shop stewards meeting with management once a month. He says: "I don't want a lot of people around here trying to represent my employees who do not know the facts about my business." These cases, however, are exceptional. Most managements are reluctant to communicate facts about the business to the employees, and they are especially reluctant to do it through officers and committeemen of the union. Past practice of employers is not a safe guide to future practice, and one may expect a great spread in the use of unions to inform employees about the problems of business concerns.

In a few cases trade unions have been a handicap to orderly and efficient administration. Occasionally unions undertake to enforce their own decisions on matters which, under the terms of their agreement with the employer, are within the scope of management's discretion. For example, the union may set formal limits on the output of certain jobs and discipline members who produce more than this amount. Or union shop stewards or other representatives may suggest limits, or encourage the men to set their own limits.[5] The union may seek to enforce straight seniority in promotion by requiring all of its members except one (the senior employee) to refuse to bid for a given vacancy. Sometimes unions organize refusals of members to work overtime or to work on Saturdays or Sundays or on a given holiday, even though the agreement provides for penalty rates of pay for overtime and holiday work. Sometimes shop stewards undertake to veto the orders of foremen and instruct members to refuse to carry out orders which, in the opinion of the shop steward, violate the agreement between the union and the employer. Sometimes unions seek by organized slow-

---

[5] When payment is by the hour or by the day, workers quite frequently agree among themselves on what they will regard as a fair day's work. The management, of course, may have different ideas concerning how much the men should produce. Time-work contracts are defective because they are incomplete. They specify how much the men shall receive per hour, but they do not specify how much men shall produce in an hour. Quite frequently the amount of work is not specified because it is not practicable to specify it; the worker may be required to perform operations which are not easily measured. It still remains true, however, that the terms of the contract are incomplete. Naturally, the worker has as much right to enforce his ideas as to what is a fair day's work as has the manager.

Does the fact that each worker may seek to enforce his own ideas as to what is a fair day's work mean that the union is justified in setting limits on the day's work? At the time the agreement between the union and the employer is negotiated, the union is, of course, justified in bargaining over how much work the men shall do. This is as legitimate as bargaining over how much the employer shall pay. If the agreement does not cover the point, however, the union is not justified in enforcing limits by unilateral action. Matters not covered by the agreement are left to be worked out between individual workers and management — subject, of course, to the right of the worker under most agreements to make grievances of practices or decisions of management which he regards as unfair.

downs to deprive management of the discretion reserved to it under the agreement.

Another way in which unions sometimes hamper efficient administration is by requiring that the foremen belong to the same union as do the men whom they boss. In principle one has difficulty in finding fault with this practice of unions. Why should not employees and stockholders bargain over who should pick the management of the plant? Employees might refuse to work for bosses whom they do not select and whom they do not control. Property owners, on the other hand, might refuse to let their property be used except under the direction of managers whom they, the stockholders, select and control. The dispute might be settled by giving the stockholders the right to choose top management and by giving the workers the right to choose their own immediate bosses. Or the dispute might be settled by giving the stockholders, or their representatives, the right to choose all supervisors, but by requiring that certain classes of supervisors, such as foremen, belong to unions of the rank and file. Certainly employees are quite justified in being concerned about whom they work under just as the stockholders are quite properly concerned about who shall manage their property. As a practical matter, however, arrangements which require foremen to belong to unions of the rank and file interfere with efficient management and, therefore, with production, without conferring substantial benefits upon the rank and file. Hence, such arrangements usually appear to prevent the production of the maximum net output.

V

Unions and managements may get on harmoniously or they may be on more or less bad terms. The objectives of the union and of management are different. The two organizations have separate sets of leaders. The fact that men are organized may make for more effective co-operation between them and management. The unions may be an invaluable instrument, as I have pointed out, for two-way communication, keeping the management better informed about the needs and aspirations of the men, and keeping the men better informed about the problems of management. Or the union may introduce organized rivalry or conflict between the officers of management and the officers of the union. The union officers may decide that the best way to keep the union strong, to discourage factionalism among its members, and to enhance the acceptance of the officers as leaders is to foster fear and suspicion of management. Misunderstandings, disagreements, threats, fights, all may help union leaders play the role of champions to their members and may help keep the members interested in the union.

It would be interesting to grade relations between unions and employers in several thousand plants on the scale of "excellent," "good," "fair," or "bad." This has never been done, and no one knows what the results would be. Even the construction of definitions and yardsticks to guide the graders in applying such classifications would not be easily accomplished. I suspect that the proportion of plants in which the grade would be low is much greater today than it will be a few years hence. Time is required for unions and employers to learn how to get along together. The fact that there has been a fivefold increase in union membership in the last fifteen years means that there are thousands of plants in which unions and managements have not done business for very long.

The fact that relations between the union and the management in a plant may be only fair or positively bad does not mean that relations between individual employees and their supervisors are bad. The personal relations of individual employees and supervisors are, to a considerable extent, independent of the relations of the union and management. Bad relations between the union and management certainly do not help increase the output of the plant. Nevertheless, bad relations between unions and management seem frequently to have surprisingly little effect upon production. This is a matter which needs further exploration. There seem to be many plants which are highly efficient despite the fact that relations between the union and management are bad.

VI

The foregoing analysis makes plain that the potential effects of collective bargaining upon the management of business concerns for both good and bad are very great. Collective bargaining may be an arrangement through which management and workers co-operate more effectively than ever before to raise production, through which communication between management and employees is greatly improved, through which management keeps itself far better informed than ever before about the problems of its employees, and through which the employees learn more than they have ever known about the problems of the business. Or collective bargaining may be an arrangement through which unions impose wasteful make-work rules on the company and obstruct the introduction of improved equipment and processes; through which the management and the union conduct hostilities, calling each other names, engaging in recriminations, perpetuating misunderstandings, and keeping each side afraid of the other.

To a considerable extent the way in which collective bargaining works is not subject to immediate control because it is determined by certain fundamental conditions, such as whether the industry is an expanding one or a contracting one, whether labor costs are a large part or a small part of total costs, whether the employees are represented by a single industrial union or a number of craft unions, and, in the latter event, whether the craft unions are in agreement or disagreement concerning their jurisdiction, and whether the union representing the employees is a rival of other unions for the right to represent the employees either in the given plant or in other plants. Accidents of personality also profoundly affect industrial relations. Widely different characteristics help men win their way to the top of business enterprises and trade unions. Some men rise in part because they are receptive to ideas and advice, because they make friends easily and win the liking and help of other persons. Other men rise because they are tough and determined to have their way, because they have clearly defined purposes and will not be balked by obstacles. Men of the former type are much more likely to have good labor relations, either as representatives of management or as representatives of unions, than men of the latter type. Any important unsolved problem is likely to be an obstacle to good labor relations. For example, the settlement of a serious jurisdictional dispute between two unions or the clearing up of a political situation within a union or within management, or the improvement of the competitive position of the company may result in a general and substantial improvement in relations between the union and management.

Despite the many conditions which affect the operation of collective bargaining and which are not easily susceptible of control, much can be done to make collective bargaining work more satisfactorily as a method of adjusting the interests of consumers in the production of goods and as an instrument for improving managerial practices. A general clarification of the rights and duties of trade unions and employers under trade agreements would help. So would a careful statement of the standards which a good agreement should meet. In addition, management, trade unions, and government could all help. Let us look into these possibilities one by one.

VII

Clarification of the rights and duties of unions and employers under trade agreements will help avoid misunderstandings and thus make for better relations. When a union and an employer enter into an agreement, each submits to certain restrictions on its freedom. The general presumption is that, except as the parties are specifically bound by the agreement, they retain the freedoms which they had before the agreement. Likewise, except as the parties have rights specifically given them by the agreement, they have no more rights than before. These generalizations, however, are subject to some qualifications. Some rights are implied in trade agreements, either because of the nature of the rights or because of established practices, and some actions are prohibited by implication if not by plain direction. There are other actions which, though not prohibited by the agreement, will not, as a matter of policy, be done or which, if done, will only be done in a certain way. The following are a few important points which frequently need clarification:

1. In the absence of a specific authorization in the agreement, do representatives of the union have the right to waive a provision of the agreement without the assent of workers who might claim valuable rights under it? Cases are bound to arise in which literal following of the agreement would produce gross inequities either to the employer or to certain groups of workers. As a general rule, trade agreements do not specifically authorize anyone to waive provisions under which workers might claim rights. Nevertheless, in some industries the custom of making such waivers may be regarded as having been established. This is a matter which needs clarification.

2. May the union endeavor to control the operation of the plant by union rules which govern the conduct of its members as employees, provided such rules do not conflict with specific provisions in the agreement? For example, in the absence of an understanding that the union will not limit output, may the union fine men for producing more than a certain amount? May the union seek to enforce straight seniority in promotions by inducing all members except the senior one to refuse to bid for a given vacancy? Here again there is ambiguity where there ought to be clarity. The union which does these things plainly seems to have exceeded its rights because it is attempting by indirection to impose restrictions on the management of the plant which are not contained in the agreement.

3. Should the management expect the union to help it in improving production? The answer to this question seems to be "No." The employer may *persuade* the union to help, and the union may be glad to do this as a matter of good will and co-operation. If the employer is having trouble in meeting competition, the local union may regard helping management raise output as a good way of helping its members hold their jobs. Responsibility for production, however, belongs to management, and the union is under no *obligation* to help management to do its job.

4. Should the union help management maintain discipline? The answer to this question depends upon whether discipline is imposed because of a violation of shop rules or because of a violation of the agreement. The management is responsible for enforcing its

own shop rules. The union cannot be regarded as having the obligation to help management perform this job. The union officers may as a matter of good will and co-operation be willing to assist management by warning this or that worker that continued infraction of shop rules may get him into trouble. Furthermore, the management as a matter of policy may seek to give the union a chance to keep its members out of trouble by informing the union representative that a given worker is violating rules and that continued violation will lead to discipline.

Very different is the problem raised when employees violate the terms of the agreement between the employer and the union. In such cases the employee must be regarded as doing something against the union as well as against the employer. In such cases the union may see fit to act on its own initiative and to impose its own discipline on the employee. Suppose, however, that the employer asks the union representatives to help discover the ringleader in a sit-down strike or in a slow-down. Are the union representatives under an obligation to help? If the union officers know who were the ringleaders, should they tell the employer? Should they tell him if he asks them?

Opinions on these questions will differ. My judgment is that the union officers are entitled to use their discretion, just as the management is entitled to use its discretion in deciding when to impose discipline and how severe to make the discipline. Thus, the union may see fit to impose discipline itself rather than to help the employer impose it. Union officers, however, should recognize that violations of the agreement are an offense against the union as well as against the employer. They should recognize that they have the responsibility to keep such offenses to a minimum. Their attitude should not be merely one of "let the employer do it." In every instance the union officials should seek to determine who was responsible for bringing about a violation of the agreement. Furthermore, the minimum action which the union representatives should take is to warn the culprits and to make plain that a repetition of the offense will lead to discipline by the union or a request by the union that the employer impose discipline.

5. Is it proper for a management, in the absence of specific restrictions in the agreement, to make changes in the shop rules which affect the employees? The answer to this question seems to be "Yes," provided, of course, the changes do not seek by indirection to take away rights conferred on the workers by the agreement or to put into effect conditions which are specifically prohibited by the agreement. The management, in bargaining away its discretion on certain points, does not bargain away its discretion on other points not covered by the agreement. Many agreements, of course, give the union the right to challenge under the grievance machinery any new rules which the employees regard as unfair. As a matter of policy, managements will be wise to consult both union representatives and foremen before putting new shop rules into effect. Not only will consultation give management useful criticisms and suggestions, but it will promote better relations

by giving the union a sense of security and by avoiding unpleasant surprises which are bound to disturb and antagonize union representatives.

6. May a management on its own initiative and without consulting the union give wage increases, bonuses, pensions, or vacation rights over and above those provided in the agreement? For example, if the management has difficulty in obtaining certain types of labor at the rates provided in the agreement, may the management offer more than the stipulated minimum? May the management put in a Christmas bonus? May the management offer a vacation plan when the union has not negotiated one? May the management adopt a pension plan or put into effect liberalized pension payments?

Some decisions of the National Labor Relations Board hold that unilateral action of management in these matters may be a refusal to bargain and, therefore, an unfair labor practice. This view seems to me to be of doubtful validity as a general proposition. If the action of the employer in giving the men better conditions is part of a general plan to undermine the union, it may certainly be held to be an unfair labor practice on the ground that it interferes with the self-organization of workers. The mere undertaking by an employer to meet competition or to be generous should not be regarded as an unfair labor practice. At the expiration of the agreement the union would, of course, have an opportunity to bargain over any changes in wages, bonuses, vacation plans, or pensions. The essence of the bargain between the union and the employer, however, is that for the duration of the agreement both the employer and the union have agreed to certain restrictions and have also bargained to retain certain freedoms. It is a narrow and unrealistic conception of union-employer relations which requires that minimum rates of pay be maximum rates, which deprives employers of the right to meet competition in the labor market, and which even deprives them of the right to be generous if they so desire. If an enterprise has done well and wishes to share some of its prosperity by telling all employees to take an extra week's vacation or by liberalizing the pension plan, the management is surely free to do it. It is childish to argue that the employer must not be generous because he might diminish the prestige of the union. The union which would lose prestige because the employer is generous is not worthy of prestige anyway.

A sharp distinction should be made, however, between what employers have the right to do and what, as a matter of policy, they should do or how, as a matter of policy, they should proceed. Employers who wish to be generous would do well to consult the union in advance, to seek its suggestions, and to invite its criticisms and specific proposals. The union representatives are a valuable source of information about the problems and preferences of employees. A wise management will not act without getting the benefit of advice from this rich source of information.

VIII

The potential contribution of collective bargaining to better management can be more completely realized if agreements meet certain standards of a "good" agreement. Little has been done to define what tests a "good" agreement should meet. The general principle is that it should contain compromises which recognize the most crucial interests of both the union and the management. The following are the principal conditions which a "good" agreement should meet:

1. It should give security to the union.

2. It should give management reasonable opportunity to select its own employees.

3. It should protect management from being required to discharge valuable employees because of the imposition of discipline by the union unless the discipline has been reviewed by the same umpire who reviews discipline imposed by management.

4. It should give management reasonable freedom to make changes in methods and equipment.

5. It should give workers reasonable protection from technological changes.

6. It should not enforce wasteful utilization of labor.

7. It should provide an orderly way of allocating work in the event of a drop in the demand for labor by the enterprise. It should protect the workers from permanent layoff because of temporary declines in the demand for labor.

8. It should permit management to retain reasonable incentives to encourage efficiency.

9. It should provide machinery for determining the meaning of the agreement in the event of disputes over its interpretation and for enforcing the agreement in the event of violation by the employer or by the union.

10. It should provide machinery for hearing grievances which do not arise out of alleged violations of the agreement but which arise because the employer or the union is acting in ways which the other regards as unfair.

These specifications of a "good" agreement require little comment. The need of the union for security is obvious. So also is the importance to the employer of the right to select his own employees and of not being required to hire people whom he may not wish as employees. I have pointed out earlier in this chapter that it is part of the management's skill to determine who is best fitted for a given job. The employer also has an interest that the arbitrary imposition of discipline by the union shall not deprive him of valuable employees. All of these interests can be satisfied by a union-shop (not a closed-shop) agreement which requires that men join the union after a probationary period but which relieves the employer of the obligation to discharge any worker who has lost his good standing in the union unless the union's action in disciplining the employee has been upheld by the umpire who reviews allegations of unfair discipline by the employer.

The need of managements for freedom to make changes in methods and equipment is also self-evident. In a rapidly changing world survival occurs by adaptation. Hence, provisions in the agreement which restrict the employer's efforts to adapt his business to changing conditions should be kept to a minimum. Managements, however, should not expect to be free to make technological changes without undertaking to give workers reasonable protection from such changes. They should assume the obligation either to train the displaced men for other work and transfer them to it or to pay them a dismissal wage. Managements should be permitted, however, to hire temporary workers to fill jobs which are soon to be eliminated by changes.

Avoiding the wasteful use of labor is an obligation which both the employer and the union owe to the community. The employer may be able to pass on to consumers the cost of make-work rules, but this does not alter the fact that such rules lower the standard of living of the community by limiting the amount which the labor force is permitted to produce. Regulation of the manner in which employment shall be distributed in slack times introduces some measure of certainty into the lives of millions of workers and is of great importance. If decreases in the demand for labor are met by layoffs, men should ordinarily be dropped in accordance with strict seniority. Otherwise no worker knows where he stands. If layoffs are based upon strict seniority or if layoffs are avoided by dividing the work among all employees, it becomes particularly important that promotions be based upon merit rather than upon seniority. Otherwise the management is too completely deprived of incentives to stimulate efficiency among the force.

Particularly important are arrangements for interpreting the agreement. Unless an umpire is provided for in the agreement itself, the employer in most instances is in a position to enforce his own interpretation — unless the union sees fit to strike in violation of the agreement or to appeal to the courts as it probably could in some states. In the United States there are still a few unions and employers who prefer not to submit the interpretation of their agreements to neutrals, but the number is diminishing. Some agreements seem to assume that the responsibility of the neutral is merely to declare the meaning of disputed clauses. This leaves the ways and means of enforcing the agreement quite ambiguous. Fortunately, the problem does not frequently arise, possibly because most questions on the meaning of agreements are raised by actions of employers and because unions are usually willing to strike, if necessary, to compel the employer to accept the umpire's decision. This leaves unsolved the problem of enforcing the agreement against workers or the unions. Umpires should have specific authority to enforce the agreement against either the employer or the employees.

How broad should be the jurisdiction of the umpire? Some people think that the union should have the right to challenge only the actions of management which are claimed to violate the agreement. Others believe that unions should have the right to challenge any action of management which is regarded as unfair. They argue that the umpire should have authority to pass on any issue concerning which the union has relinquished the right to strike. Other people hold that the union should have the right to make grievances of either alleged violations of the agreement or alleged unfair acts of management, but should have the right to carry to the umpire only the first type of case.

Certainly union representatives should have the opportunity to protest through regular channels all the way to top management any act or omission which the employees regard as unfair. Nevertheless, some restriction is needed on the type of case which may be carried to the umpire. If *any* action of management which the union regarded as unfair could be vetoed by the umpire, the direction of the business would be transferred to the umpire. Not the president of the company but the umpire would have the final decision as to whether or not a given policy should be executed. The jurisdiction of the umpire, however, should be broad enough to enable him to do more than interpret the meaning of words in a legalistic way. He should be in a position to pass on the reasonableness or fairness of many actions of management: on the fairness of new rates and job standards, on whether management has made a reasonable effort to find appropriate jobs for men displaced by technological change, on whether discipline has been reasonably severe. Unless the union has a good opportunity to challenge many actions of management, it will not be willing to permit management broad opportunity to act as it sees fit, subject to challenge by the union.

IX

What can management do to make collective bargaining produce a more satisfactory balance between the interests of consumers and the interests of employees and to contribute more effectively to the better administration of business enterprises? The following are several important contributions which management can make:

1. Help the union feel secure; in other words, make plain to the members that the management has no desire to discourage membership in it. Any fears on the part of the union members or officers that management will discourage membership will greatly increase pressure to limit or destroy management's discretion in hiring or making layoffs, transfers, or promotions. Such fears will also cause the union to seek to win the support of workers by arousing fear of management and antagonism toward it.

2. Make the job of the union representative as easy and pleasant as possible by dealing with him promptly in a matter-of-fact way, making an effort to get to the bottom of cases quickly, and disposing of them without unnecessary delay. This, of course, does not assure that the union representatives will be easy to deal with. The better the service that he is able to give his members, however, the greater his prestige with them and the less the danger that he will have to foster trouble in order to stand in with a radical minority in the union.

3. Give the union a chance to straighten out an employee who is failing to observe shop rules or who is producing work of poor quality. Management can do this by warning the shop steward of the man's deficiencies. If the employee fails to observe the warnings of the shop steward, the steward is in a better position to refuse to plead the man's case when discipline is imposed.

4. Keep the union well informed about the business and the plans of the company. Perhaps the most fre-

quent mistake which employers make in the field of labor policy is not to tell the union officers and members enough about the business. The greater the importance which both management and union attach to common interests, the greater is the likelihood that they will work out trade agreements and interpretations of trade agreements which are satisfactory to both. I venture to repeat my reference to the manufacturer in the Middle West who insists that the shop stewards meet with management once a month because he does not wish people trying to represent his employees who do not know the facts about his business. Certainly union representatives cannot be expected to know about the employer's problems unless the employer is willing to inform them.

5. Seek the help of the union in encouraging good attendance, good production, good quality. Do not confine the union to the narrow negative role of policing the agreement.

6. Consult the union representatives before putting into effect new policies or rules which affect the employees. Invite criticisms of the proposals and suggestions for improving them from the union representatives.

7. Be prepared to back decisions of management with facts and to show how and why management reached its decisions. Be ready to consider facts and arguments offered in criticism of management's decisions. Be unimpressed by oratory, table pounding, or threats.

8. Do not reward violations of the agreement by yielding to men who engage in "wild-cat" strikes or

slow-downs. Be prepared even at great expense to assert the rights given management by the trade agreement with the union. Any other course is expensive in the long run. The issues which produce wild-cat strikes or slow-downs should go to the umpire unless withdrawn by the union and should not be heard by the arbitrator until the question of discipline for the participants in the wild-cat strike or the slow-down has been settled.

9. Do not "short circuit" the union. If the management intends to introduce benefits not required by the agreement, seek the advice of the union and make the announcement jointly with the union.

10. Do not let misstatements by the union about the company or the management pass unnoticed. Public reply is usually both unnecessary and undesirable. The author or publisher of the misstatements, however, should be called in for a conference and given the facts. This policy will usually lead to union representatives' learning to inform themselves properly before making statements about the company or management.

X

What can unions do to make collective bargaining contribute more satisfactorily to a better balance between the interests of consumers and of employees and to better management of business concerns?

1. Know the long-run interests of the union members and see that the members know their long-run interests. A few leaders of unions are extremely well informed concerning the economies of the industries in which

they operate. Unfortunately most leaders have very limited knowledge of the economic problems of their industries. In particular, many union leaders are inadequately informed concerning the competitive position of their industries. Nevertheless, union officers are usually better able to see long-run consequences of given policies than is the individual member. Hence unions should be an influence for helping members to take a broader and longer view of their interests than they would take if left solely to themselves. Union leaders, for example, should be a powerful influence in advising members against insisting upon make-work rules because, at best, make-work rules give the union members only a temporary benefit and because in the long run a large part of the cost of such rules falls on the members themselves.

2. Avoid building loyalty to the unions by fostering misunderstanding between workers and management and by endeavoring to arouse fear and hatred of management. Most managements are good enough and fair enough so that efforts of union leaders to "smear" them backfire and undermine the confidence of the rank and file in their own union leaders. Furthermore, this tactic makes the management distrust the union and hold aloof from it, thereby limiting the possibility of the union representatives' developing useful contacts with the management.

3. Invite the management to inform shop stewards concerning employees who are failing to do satisfactory work so that the steward can investigate such cases, warn the employee if such action seems indicated, or

protest to the management if that action seems appropriate.

4. Develop the union into an effective agency of communication between workers and management by training shop stewards in the work of investigating and presenting grievances and by training special representatives to make technical criticisms of time studies, rates, job standards, job evaluations.

5. Welcome opportunities to co-operate with management in improving quantity and quality of production.

XI

What can the government do to make collective bargaining establish a better balance between the consideration given the interests of consumers and the interests of producers and contribute effectively to the better management of business concerns?

I have said that the method of letting bargaining power determine the rights and duties of management and the rights and duties of employees impresses one as a primitive arrangement. Of course, the rights and duties of the employers and workers are not left solely to bargaining power. The common law requires that the employer furnish a reasonably safe and sanitary place of work, and this law has been much amplified by factory legislation and by orders of commissions. Factory legislation in turn has been supplemented by the Wagner Act and the Fair Employment Standards Act, which place restrictions on management in order to give minimum rights to workers.

Thus far the government has not seen fit to police the terms of trade agreements and to forbid certain types of provisions on the ground that they are contrary to public policy. The government has relied upon the bargaining power of each side to keep burdensome and unreasonable provisions out of agreements. It is doubtful, however, whether the government will be justified in adhering indefinitely to this extreme policy of *laissez faire*. Employers may prefer to make concessions which reduce the productivity of industry and thus reduce the standard of living of the community, passing on the increase in cost to consumers. Two steps might well be taken by the government to protect the community:

1. Protection of the integrity of management by forbidding unions of rank and file employees from requiring membership on the part of supervisory employees or from representing supervisory employees.

2. Provision of a procedure by which alleged make-work rules or rules which obstruct technological change might be challenged on the ground that they are contrary to public policy.

Thurman Arnold has suggested that make-work rules or unreasonable impediments on technological change be made restraints of trade within the meaning of the Sherman Antitrust Law. This procedure involves difficulties. The Sherman Act is a criminal statute. It is not easy to draw the line between compelling the use of wasteful labor and protecting men against unreasonable and excessive job loads. In each instance, the reasonableness of the rule is at issue. Likewise, it is not easy to determine when a restriction on technological change is reasonably required to control the rate at which men are displaced and when it unreasonably deprives the community of the benefits of technological progress.

Although there is abundant precedent for imposing criminal liability when reasonable standards are ignored, this procedure should be avoided if possible. Men should be able to know definitely whether or not they are committing crimes. What is needed is an orderly way of determining whether make-work rules or restrictions on technological progress are reasonable or unreasonable. Senator Morse of Oregon has suggested that the National Labor Relations Board be given authority to issue orders against union programs to enforce the wasteful use of labor, orders which would be enforceable in the courts. A better procedure, in my judgment, would be to authorize consumers, employers, or other unions to ask the U. S. Conciliation Service to appoint a board of inquiry from its panel of arbitrators to determine whether a provision in a trade agreement unreasonably compels wasteful use of labor or unreasonably restricts technological progress. If the provision were found to be an unreasonable burden on production, continued enforcement of the rule would subject the employer, the members of management as individuals, the union, and the union members to the penalties of the Sherman Act.

XII

One must concede, after reviewing the provisions of trade agreements, that collective bargaining in general has done a good job in bringing about a better balance in the consideration given the interests of consumers and the interests of employees in the process of production. One must concede also that collective bargaining has stimulated more alert and dynamic management and better managerial practices more frequently than it has hampered management and interfered unduly with managerial discretion. The most important potentialities of collective bargaining for business management, however, are still to be realized. They are better communication between employees and management and better understanding of each other's problems. Relatively little progress has been made in this matter, but one may confidently predict that it will be made.

It is of the utmost importance to the country that better communication between unions and managements be established and that each learn far more about the problems of the other. A community in which trade unions and employers are separated by a wide gulf, in which they call each other names in a reckless fashion, in which they do not appreciate the importance of their common interests or understand the problems of each other is in a dangerous condition. Its capacity to deal with its problems in a matter-of-fact and informed manner is limited; its institutions have a less favorable chance of working satisfactorily and, therefore, of surviving. It is in the hundreds of thousands of shops, mines, railroads, warehouses, and retail stores throughout the country that understanding between employees and managements must be built up. Leadership can be given by the national heads of unions and by the representatives of organized employers. The real spade work, however, must be done in the individual plants. The prospects that it will be done is one of the brightest aspects of the economic future of America.

Chapter III

The Economic Consequences of

the Wage Policies of Unions

I

When fifteen million workers band together into over 50,000 local unions and over 190 national unions, can they by sheer bargaining might raise the standard of living of the nation? Or do unions by imposing stiff terms on industry limit employment and production, and thus reduce the standard of living of the country? Even if unions reduce the standard of living of the nation, may they nevertheless raise the standard of living of their own members? If so, at the expense of what part of the community do the organized workers make their gains? If unions tend to diminish the standard of living as a whole, can anything be done to avert this effect? If they tend to introduce inequities into the distribution of income, can anything be done to prevent that?

As I pointed out in the first chapter, most wage earners have unquestioned faith in bargaining power as a device for raising the income of labor. They take it for granted that a higher price for labor will produce larger payrolls. They also take it for granted that payrolls can

[71]

be increased by encroaching on profits. The faith of workers in bargaining goes far beyond these assumptions. Many workers believe that if too large a share of income goes to profits, the economy will collapse. Hence, they believe that wages must be constantly pushed up through the bargaining power of unions in order to maintain the stability of the economy.

All of these assumptions, which are taken as self-evident truths by millions of workers, are open to question and are at best true only under certain conditions. Let us look first at the effect of unions on the standard of living of the entire community, and then let us look at the effect of unions upon the standard of living of their own members.

II

Total output of goods divided by population of the community gives the average standard of living for the community. The effect of unions upon the output of goods depends upon how they affect:

1. The efficiency of management.
2. The structure of wages.
3. The movement of wages.
4. The rate of technological discovery and the rate at which discoveries are put into effect.

In the last chapter I discussed the effect of collective bargaining upon management, and I reached the conclusion (1) that in most industries it had produced a better adjustment between the interests of consumers, as represented by management, and the interests of employees—that is, an adjustment which yields a larger net output than would have resulted from individual bargaining — and (2) that it had stimulated better administration. Let us look next at the effect of collective bargaining upon the structure of wages — that is, upon the relative levels of wage rates in different occupations, industries, and places.

The structure of wages produced by collective bargaining is unfavorable to the achievement of the largest net national output for two reasons. One reason is that the wage structure created by collective bargaining prevents industry from producing goods in the most advantageous proportions — the most advantageous "product-mix," the "right" number of automobiles in relation to the number of mattresses, hogs, razors, shoes, and everything else. The other reason is that the wage structure created by collective bargaining produces "wage-distortion unemployment" and thus limits the output of industry.

In order for industry to turn out the product-mix which yields the greatest satisfaction to consumers in relation to the cost of producing it, wages in different occupations, industries, and places must be such as to equalize the attractiveness of jobs requiring the same degrees of skill and responsibility. This means that wages for the same type of labor should not be the same in different occupations, industries, or places but should vary inversely with the attractiveness of the occupation, industry, or place. Collective bargaining, however, cannot be expected to produce a wage structure which equalizes the attractiveness of jobs requiring the same type of labor. The wage structure developed under collective bargaining must be expected to reflect the bargaining power of the different groups of workers and the different employers with whom they deal. By bargaining power in this connection I mean the ability of the union or the employer to produce a greater or less deviation of the wage of a given group of workers from the average of all wages than would exist under free markets.[1] In industries, occupations, or places where unions are very strong, wages may be expected to be higher relative to skill and responsibility than in other industries, occupations, or places where unions are weak. As a result, prices will be higher and output less where the bargaining power of unions is high, and prices will be lower and output more where bargaining power of unions is low, than would be the case if wages were so adjusted as to equalize the attractiveness of jobs requiring men of the same or similar skill and responsibility. Under universal collective bargaining about half of the unions would have positive bargaining power and about half of them negative bargaining power — that is, half of the unions would be able to make wages higher relative to the average than wages would be under free markets, and half of the unions would not be able to push wages so high.

---

[1] Bargaining power can and should be defined in broader terms than this. In general the bargaining power of a group is its power to affect the price, or prices, at which the group buys or sells. It manifests itself in various ways; in the case of trade unions, for example, partly in the responsiveness of union wage rates to changes in the demand for labor. Bargaining power may be defined in terms of the ability of the group to affect certain *prices* (such as the price of labor) or in terms of the ability of the group to affect *incomes*, the average annual earnings of members of the group, for example, or the total wage income of all members of the group.

All of this means that under collective bargaining goods will not be produced in the proportions which will maximize the net national product. In industries and places where the unions have sufficient bargaining power to raise their wages higher above the general mean level of wages than free markets would set those wages, the output of goods will be too small. In industries and places where the bargaining power of unions is so weak that wages are lower relative to the general level of wages than would be the case in free markets, the output of goods under collective bargaining will be too large. The unfavorable effect upon the national product is probably not great. There is no way of measuring it. Nevertheless, it would be surprising if the output of more than one-third of the work force were seriously affected. If the product of this portion of the work force were one-fourth less desirable on the average than their output would be under free labor markets, the total national product would be diminished by less than one-tenth.

Incidentally, when one asks how collective bargaining alters the dispersion of wage rates around the general average of wages, one notes that, when collective bargaining becomes fairly universal, the real bargaining will be in the main between unions and unions. Through the media of employers, unions will bargain with one another over the division of the 60 per cent and more of the national income which goes to employees. The strong unions will enforce wages and terms of employment which compel the employers to charge relatively high prices, which the members of weak unions and their families must pay. That universal collective bargaining would boil down largely to bargaining between unions has escaped attention because until recently unions have been only a small part of the community. Hence, their bargains have affected unorganized workers more than other union workers.

The fact that collective bargaining produces a wage structure which reflects the relative bargaining power of unions and employers rather than the skill and responsibilities of workers means that it also produces wage-distortion unemployment. This type of unemployment exists because wage rates in industries, occupations, and places in which unions are especially strong are unusually attractive to workers and draw to those industries, occupations, and places more people than are needed to meet the demand. If the wages are sufficiently high, a worker will remain attached to an industry, occupation, or place even though he is able to pick up only 150 or 175 days of work in the course of a year rather than shift to another industry, occupation, or place where at lower wages he might pick up 250 or 275 days of work in a year. Examples of this were found in the needle trades before the war. Strong and well-run unions had done much to increase the attractiveness of these industries. The dollar output of women's and children's apparel, for example, dropped from 1.4 billion dollars in 1923 to 1.3 billion dollars in 1939; but the number of wage earners more than doubled, rising from 133,195 to 279,402. In the men and boys' clothing industry, dollar output dropped sharply from 1 billion dollars in 1923 to 681 million dollars in 1939; but the number of wage earners increased slightly from 158,173 in 1923 to 161,731 in 1939. The increase in workers relative to jobs is reflected in the reduction of the average annual take-home compensation of workers, which, in the production of women's and children's apparel dropped from $1,324 in 1923 to $920 in 1939, and in the production of men's and boys' clothing from $1,311 in 1923 to $971 in 1939. When more people are attracted to an industry than can find steady work, the national income is, of course, being limited by unemployment.

III

What is the effect of collective bargaining upon the movement of wages? For several generations output per man-hour in the United States has been rising at the rate of about 2 per cent a year. Perhaps it will rise at a faster rate for some years to come, say at the rate of 3 per cent a year. Let us assume that collective bargaining becomes fairly universal and that unions are not content to raise wages at the rate of only 3 per cent a year and that they insist upon pushing up wages at the rate of 5 per cent a year. What will happen? Will prices rise sufficiently to offset the difference between the rate at which unions raise wages and the rate at which the managers and engineers are able to raise output per man-hour? If prices do not rise sufficiently to offset the difference, will there be unemployment?

Many economists believe that any tendency for collective bargaining to raise wages faster than output per man-hour increases will be offset by a rise in prices.[2] Consequently, in the view of these economists, collective bargaining cannot raise wages relative to prices. All that it can do is to cause wage-price relationships to adjust themselves to technological progress through a rise in money wages rather than through a fall in prices. Many workers (possibly most workers), on the other hand, not only believe that collective bargaining can raise wages relative to prices, but also believe that pushing up wages relative to prices is good for employment and, in fact, that it is necessary in order to prevent depressions.

The view that a rise of money wages which exceeds the rise in output per man-hour will produce an offsetting rise in prices rests upon assumptions which are unrealistic in the extreme. A rise in money wages can produce an offsetting rise in prices only if there is a rise in expenditures for goods or a drop in the production of goods. A rise in expenditures can occur only if there is either an increase in the supply of money or an increase in willingness to spend money. Can a rise in labor costs be counted upon to produce precisely the increase in the supply of money or in the willingness to spend money required to raise prices by the same

---

[2] This view is expressed by some followers of Keynes who have erroneously attributed it to him. Mrs. Joan Robinson, for example, in her *Introduction to the Theory of Employment* (pp. 50–51) says:

"If entrepreneurs agree to pay their workers higher rates, money demand for goods is increased, and it is argued from this that activity and output will increase. But this rise in demand merely offsets the rise in the cost of production due to higher wages. A larger expenditure of money is now needed to buy the same goods and the increase in money income is not an increase in real purchasing power."

amount as the rise in labor costs? An increase in labor costs might produce some rise in the supply of money because it might increase the need of business concerns for working capital and thus bring about an expansion of bank credit. Higher labor costs might produce some increase in spending by business concerns, at least a rise in spending for direct labor, but higher labor costs would also cause the execution of some business plans to be postponed until it became clear whether or not prices would rise to offset the advance in costs. This would tend to prevent any rise in prices. Hence, an increase in labor costs might produce no rise in prices at all. At any rate, it would be an extraordinary coincidence if the supply of money and the willingness to spend money were to increase by exactly enough to raise prices no more and no less than the rise in labor costs.[3] This analysis indicates that advances in labor costs cannot be counted upon to produce offsetting increases in the price level.

The effect of union wage policy upon prices varies with different phases of the business cycle. Before reaching a final conclusion concerning the long-run response

---

[3] Mr. Abba Lerner has attempted to show that the rise in spending by an amount exactly sufficient to raise prices by the amount of the increase in labor costs would not be a coincidence. Until an offsetting rise in prices has occurred, says Mr. Lerner, there will be an expansion. "As long as employment is less than before, the community will want to save less than is being invested, the difference showing itself in unintended savings of business out of unexpected profits" (*American Economic Review, Supplement,* May, 1946, p. 331). Mr. Lerner's argument ignores the fact that changes in costs relative to prices produce a greater shift in the savings function and in the investment function. Only as a matter of accident will the equilibrium point produced by the new functions be the same as the equilibrium point produced by the original functions.

of prices to upward pressure of unions upon wages, one should analyze the effect of union wage policy at different phases of the business cycle.[4] During periods of revival and during much of the period of booms, wage increases are readily passed on to consumers in the form of advances in prices. During a depression a certain amount of demand accumulates, and much of this demand in the course of time becomes fairly urgent. Furthermore, rising prices produce a certain amount of anticipatory buying. This also helps business concerns pass on rising costs in the form of higher prices.

The demand which accumulates during a depression, however, is limited. So also is the amount of buying which enterprises and individuals are willing to do in anticipation of higher prices. As the boom develops, business concerns eventually find growing difficulty

---

[4]The cyclical movements of prices have preceded the cyclical movements of wages. Wages may be moving downward for six months or a year after prices start moving upward, but when prices move downward at the end of the boom, wages may drop little or not at all. Union wages have apparently moved upward more slowly than nonunion wages during the period of boom. But they have continued rising during depressions after nonunion wages have started to fall. Over a period of a number of business cycles, union wages and nonunion wages seem to have increased by about the same rate.

Douglas found that among factory workers "payroll" hourly earnings increased 3.27 times between 1890 and 1926 and that the hourly earnings of union workers in manufacturing increased by substantially the same amount, 3.11 times. "Payroll" hourly earnings represent industries in which there were both nonunion and union workers, but mostly nonunion (P. H. Douglas, *Real Wages in the United States*, pp. 96–102). The union hourly earnings do not pertain to the same occupations and industries as do the payroll data, and the union data apply to more skilled workers than do the payroll data. For these reasons the comparison leaves much to be desired.

in passing on rising costs in the form of higher prices. The bargaining power of trade unions increases, however, and unemployment is less. Further, the pressure of members for higher wages is likely to grow. Hence, unions are likely to insist on wage increases after wage increases can no longer be easily passed on in the form of higher prices. This upward pressure on costs may help bring the boom to a conclusion and produce a recession. Experience shows that unions are able to push up wages for a considerable period after business has turned down. This encroachment of wages upon profits will discourage long-term business planning and accentuate the recession.

During periods of depression unions prevent wages from falling as much as they would fall in free markets. The effect of union wage policies upon the severity of depressions is in doubt. In the case of raw materials produced by farmers rather than by wage earners, the maintenance of wages in industries which use the raw materials tends to depress the price of the raw materials, in accordance with the familiar principle that a rise in the supply price of one complementary good diminishes the demand for the other complementary good. On the other hand, the maintenance of wages does good by creating the belief that prices are too low in relation to costs and that they must go higher. One would attach considerably more importance to this favorable effect did not the support of wages by unions during the depression involve not merely the support of the wage *level* but also support of whatever maladjustments in the wage *structure* may have developed during the preceding boom.

When one considers the effect of union wage policy upon prices in all phases of the business cycle, does one conclude that prices may be expected to rise sufficiently to offset any tendency for wages to advance faster than output per man-hour? The answer is in doubt, and probably depends upon whether the support of wages by unions during depressions diminishes or increases the severity of depressions. If the former, union upward pressure on wages may well produce an offsetting secular rise in prices. On the other hand, if union wage policy makes depressions more severe, the secular rise in prices cannot be expected to be sufficient to offset the rise in labor costs. In that event will not unemployment increase until the bargaining power of unions becomes so weak that they are not able to raise wages faster than the managers and the engineers raise output per man-hour?

IV

Many wage earners and some union leaders believe that raising wages faster than the increase in output per man-hour is good for employment. They argue that higher wages would mean larger payrolls, that larger payrolls would mean larger consumer purchasing power, that larger consumer purchasing power would mean an increase in investment, and that the net result would be a gain in employment.

This argument obviously assumes too much and proves too much. For example, whether higher wages will mean larger or smaller payrolls depends upon how much they affect employment. But the effect upon employment of wage increases which are not offset by higher prices or higher output per man-hour is the question at issue. The answer to the question must not be assumed in the analysis. The argument also assumes too much because it assumes that an increase in payrolls, if it occurs, also produces an expansion of investment. *Any* shifts in income which change the kind of goods demanded will produce a momentary rise in investment opportunities because the plant of industry will be adjusted to the new pattern of demand. The rise in investment opportunities, however, is only a momentary one because the opportunities will be extinguished as soon as the adjustments in plant have been made. The long-run supply of investment opportunities will depend (1) upon the rate at which technological discoveries are being made and (2) upon the relationship of costs to prices.

The basic issue raised by the proposition that higher wages relative to prices will increase employment is whether an encroachment upon profits will reduce the propensity to save more than it reduces the supply of investment opportunities. Both the volume of saving and, to a less extent, the volume of investment opportunities vary with the level of the national income. Likewise, they both vary with wage-price relationships. Since a larger fraction of profits is saved than of wages, the higher wages are in relation to profits, the smaller will be the volume of savings at any given level of income. Likewise, the higher wages are in relation to prices, the smaller will be the fraction of technological discoveries which will yield a given return and hence the smaller the volume of investment opportunities at any given level of income. Given supply prices for investment-seeking funds, one can construct a series of curves showing for each level of national income the volume of investment opportunities and the volume of savings which will exist under different cost-price relationships. In each case the level of income payments will be determined at the intersection of the appropriate curves showing the volume of savings and the volume of investment opportunities — the savings function and the investment function.

A rise in wages relative to prices will produce a favorable shift in the savings function and an unfavorable shift in the investment function. Obviously the crucial question is whether the favorable shift in the savings function is smaller than or greater than the unfavorable shift in the investment function. If the rise in wages relative to prices produces a greater shift in the investment function than in the savings function, the volume of income payments will drop and *pro tanto* the volume of employment will drop also. If the shift in the savings function is greater than the shift in the investment function, income payments will rise. If they rise more than the price of labor has advanced, the volume of employment will increase.

Persons who assert that employment will be increased by a rise in wages are asserting that the savings function is more sensitive to changes in wage-price relationships than the investment function. This may be true, but the evidence points to the opposite conclusion—at least within the range of wage-price relationships furnished by experience. One bit of evidence is the fact that costs which are so high relative to prices as to destroy all investment opportunities would not necessarily prevent all saving. Another bit of evidence is the fact that the fluctuations of employment, income, and prices are not very pronounced. If changes in labor costs relative to prices produce smaller shifts in the investment function than in the savings function, one would expect the economy to be subject to greater extremes of inflation or deflation. A rise in wages relative to prices would increase the demand for labor and this would produce another rise in wages relative to prices and another increase in the demand for labor. Decreases in wages relative to prices would be equally cumulative in their effects. Once the economy got started going up or going down, only very powerful external events would produce a turning point. This does not seem to be the kind of economy in which we live. Consequently, one must infer that changes in costs relative to prices produce greater shifts in the savings function than in the investment function.

V

Many people, who do not believe that higher wages would immediately increase employment by raising the proportion of incomes spent on consumption, will argue that upward pressure on wages from unions is needed to help the economy adjust itself to technological change. If output per man-hour rises, it is argued that either prices must be reduced or wages must be raised in order to avert an increase in profits. An increase in profits, it is argued, will be deflationary because a large part of profits are saved. Business, it is said, cannot be trusted promptly to cut prices or to bid up wages as output per man-hour is increased. Hence it is stated that wages must be raised by collective bargaining in order to avert disaster. This reasoning raises several fundamental questions of great importance, such as:

1. Is it possible that prices or wages might move too rapidly in response to technological change?

2. How does the outlook for profits affect the volume of spending?

3. What is the best lag between the achievement of a reduction in production cost and a reduction in the prices of goods or a rise in wages?

4. If a lag occurs in the adjustment of prices to technological change, will the resulting rise in profits produce a rise in spending and indirectly a rise in wages?

Let us suppose that output per man-hour increases by 10 per cent. In order to prevent this rise in output from producing unemployment, either prices must drop by approximately 10 per cent or expenditures must rise by 10 per cent. It is clear that a prompt reduction in price would prevent a drop in employment because the same volume of expenditures would buy 10 per cent more goods. The prompt drop in prices, however, would prevent the rise in output per man-hour from increasing profits. Hence there would be no incentive for enterprises to make innovations. Even more unsatisfactory would be the extreme of promptly raising wages in proportion to the rise in output per man-hour. The raising of wages would not increase the total volume of spending. If wages immediately rose by 10 per cent to offset the increase in output per man-hour, labor costs would not be diminished. With unchanged costs, business enterprises would have no reason to change either prices or volume of output. If the volume of output remained unchanged, the income of wage earners as a class would be unchanged. The workers who received wage increases as a result of the rise in output per man-hour would, it is true, be receiving 10 per cent more, but the rise in efficiency would mean that 10 per cent fewer workers would be needed. The total payroll would be no greater than before the change in efficiency. The net result would be more unemployment and higher wages for the employed.

This analysis indicates that the adjustment to greater efficiency must occur in part through an increase in the rate of spending. If the response of prices or wages to increases in output per man-hour is not too rapid, technological change will raise the rate of spending because it will improve prospective profits on new investments. Better prospects for profits produce an increase in business spending (1) by leading enterprises to operate existing plants at a higher rate, (2) by leading enterprises to expand existing productive capacity, and (3) by causing new concerns to be started in industries where profits have risen. The increase in spending may be made possible by a more rapid turnover of existing bank balances or by an expansion of commercial credit. In the long run it seems to have been made possible by an expansion of bank credit rather than by an increase in the rate of spending.[5] The increase in business spending, of course, tends to raise prices in general and also the level of wages. At the same time the increase in business spending, by raising the productive capacity of the industry in which output per man-hour has increased, tends to depress the price of the goods turned out by the industry. Thus the adjustment of the economy to technological progress takes the form *both* of an increase in spending and a rise in the prices of a multitude of goods and also of a fall in the prices of the goods which are made by the new and more efficient methods. Whether the adjustment principally takes the form of more spending or of lower prices of goods made by more efficient methods depends upon how sensitive the money supply and willingness to spend money are to improvements in the prospect for profits.

Experience during the last hundred years indicates that the adjustment of the economy to greater output per man-hour has occurred more through the expansion of spending and the rise in money wages than through a drop in prices. In 1940 output per man-hour in the economy as a whole was roughly six times as great as in 1840.[6] The index of wholesale prices in 1940 was about 10 per cent higher than in 1840. The index has an upward bias, which indicates that the real level of prices in 1940 was moderately below the level of 1840. Hourly earnings outside of agriculture in 1940

---

[5]Between 1840 and 1940 the volume of bank deposits and money in circulation increased nearly six times as fast as the national income.

[6] The difficulties of measuring output per man-hour over long periods means that the above estimate is exceedingly rough.

were nearly eight times as high as in 1840. No other price series rose as rapidly as hourly earnings. Hence it is plain that the adjustment to technological change during this hundred-year period took the form of a rise in spending rather than a drop in prices.

This analysis indicates that collective bargaining is not needed to help the economy adjust itself to technological change. In fact, there is danger that collective bargaining will seriously impede adjustments to technological change. A distinction needs to be made between wage increases which occur because of the rise in the demand price for labor, the result of increases in output per man-hour, and wage increases which occur because of organized efforts to raise the supply price of labor. If unions raise the supply price of labor faster than increases in output per man-hour raise the demand for labor, unions will encroach upon profits and limit the effectiveness of profits as a device for (1) increasing the volume of spending, and (2) increasing the volume of production. Thus unions would make technological progress produce unemployment instead of more goods. In an extreme case, unions might push up the supply price of labor so promptly and so completely in response to increases in the demand for labor that, as explained above, technological progress would produce no rise in output but merely a rise in unemployment.

VI

If prices fail to rise sufficiently to offset advances in labor costs, may technological change be expected to increase sufficiently to prevent a drop in employment? Industrial research has been growing by leaps and bounds for some years. Indeed, for sixty years, the number of research workers and technological engineers has been growing from ten to fourteen times as fast as the gainfully employed. This increase started long before unions became strong, and the rise of unions cannot be regarded as having much to do with the growth of research. In the future, the research plans of many enterprises are bound to be materially affected by the great strength of unions. It is difficult, for example, to imagine that some industries will not make research plans to protect themselves from the enormous strength of the coal miners' union. Much of the response of managements to wage pressure from unions is found in the operating departments and engineering departments rather than in the research departments. It takes the form of many small changes made to keep labor costs under control. The response of technological research to the bargaining power of this or that union does not necessarily occur in the industry where the members of the union work. For example, the response to the great bargaining power of the locomotive engineers and firemen may be in the improvement of locomotives by the locomotive builders rather than in the research done by the railroads themselves.

Obviously one cannot expect industrial research to be so responsive to the bargaining power of unions that output per man-hour never rises less rapidly than money wages. Nevertheless, the tendency for collective bargaining to accelerate technological discovery is undoubtedly one of its most useful effects and goes far to offset any bad effects of collective bargaining, such as its tendency to bring about an unfavorable product-mix, to produce wage-distortion unemployment, or to limit the volume of investment opportunities. At the end of twenty years a 2 per cent annual increase in output per man-hour means a total rise of 48.6 per cent. If the pressure of unions, however, were to raise the annual rate of increase to 3 per cent, output per man-hour at the end of twenty years would have increased 80.6 per cent. If union pressure were to make the annual increase 4 per cent, the increase at the end of twenty years would be 119.1 per cent. Hence, it is plain that unions by putting pressure on management to raise output per man-hour can offset much, if not all, of the unfavorable effects which collective bargaining might have upon the standard of living of the community. Indeed, unions by stimulating technological progress may become a powerful influence for raising the standard of living of the community. If this were to happen, not all of the credit for the achievement would properly belong to the union; most of it would belong to the scientists, engineers, and managers whose imagination, ingenuity, and hard work discovered the ways of making labor more productive.

VII

Is collective bargaining a device through which employees may increase their share of the national product? May collective bargaining raise the average income of the individual union member even if it does not raise either the proportion of the national income or the absolute amount of the national income going to union members?

The effect of collective bargaining upon the share of the national income going to union members depends, in case the organization of labor is incomplete, upon the possibility of substituting nonunion labor, self-employed workers, and capital for union labor; and, in case all employees are union members, upon the possibility of substituting self-employed workers and capital for union labor. If a 10 per cent increase in the price of union labor relative to commodity prices reduces by less than 10 per cent the amount of union labor used with nonunion employees, the self-employed, and capital, the share of union members in the national income will rise; if the rise in union wages produces a more than proportionate drop in the number of union employees used with nonunion employees, self-employed workers, and capital, the share going to union members will drop.[7] These statements are important because they indicate that the mere determination of unions to push up wages and to stand long strikes, if necessary, will not enable them to increase the share of union members in the national income. Whether higher wages bring union members a larger or smaller share in the national income is beyond the control of trade unions; it depends upon the extent

---

[7] In other words, a rise in the supply price of union labor relative to other supply prices will increase the share of the national product going to union members if the elasticity of substitution is less than unity, and will diminish the share if the elasticity of substitution is greater than unity.

to which other types of labor or capital are substituted for union labor as union wage scales rise relative to other forms of compensation. When union members are about fifteen million out of a work force of sixty million, the possibility of substituting other forms of labor for union employees is undoubtedly very high. The substitution, of course, does not occur in the union plants themselves, but through the shift of business from union plants to nonunion and from the shift of buying from the products of union industries to the products of nonunion industries. Union membership, of course, might be concentrated in occupations in which the technological possibilities of replacing labor with machinery are small and in industries which make products that are inelastic in demand. Under those conditions a rise in union wages relative to other rates of compensation would increase the share of union members in the national product. These special conditions, however, must be regarded as unlikely.

As the proportion of employees who belong to unions increases, the possibilities of substituting nonunion labor for union labor diminish and the ability of unions to raise the share of the national income going to union members increases. Even in an economy in which *all* workers, except perhaps a few self-employed, were union members, the possibility of substituting capital for labor might be so high that unions would reduce rather than increase the share of labor in the national product by raising wage rates relative to interest rates. Certainly under present conditions any tendency of unions to raise wages faster than the increase in output per man-hour may be expected to reduce the share of union members in the national product. In other words, under present conditions, unions must choose between whether they wish to get the largest possible wage increase for their members or the largest possible share for their members in the national product. So long as nonunion workers and capital are easily substituted for union employees, the two objectives conflict. Unions succeed in achieving one of these objectives only at the cost of failing to achieve the other.

Even if the share of union members as a group in the national product is diminished by a rise in union wage rates faster than the gain in output per man-hour, may not the advance in union wage rates increase the average annual income of employees receiving the union wage scale relative to the incomes of the rest of the community? This will depend upon how a change in union wage scales relative to other wages and to the incomes of self-employed affects the ratio of job seekers to the number of jobs in union plants. Let us assume that at a given wage there are 1,000 job seekers for every 1,000 jobs in union plants — in other words, no unemployment. At a higher wage, there will be more than 1,000 job seekers for every 1,000 jobs. If a rise in union wages of 10 per cent produces a more than proportionate increase in the number of persons attached to the occupation or industry, unions will reduce the average annual income (exclusive of unemployment compensation) of the persons attached to the union occupations or plants; if a given rise in wages produces a less than proportionate increase in the supply of labor attached to the occupation or industry, advances in the union scale will raise the average annual income of persons who work at the union wage scale. If the ratio of job seekers to jobs rises faster than the ratio of union wage scales to other wages, unions may prevent a drop in the average annual income of their members by imposing the closed shop in union plants and restricting admission to the union.

VIII

This analysis of the effects of union wage policies upon the national income and upon the incomes of union members shows that mere pressure of unions for higher wages, even when backed by abundant union treasuries and by great willingness on the part of union members to engage in long strikes, cannot be depended upon to raise the standard of living of the community as a whole, to increase the share of the national income going to union members, or to increase the average income of union members relative to the incomes of other members of the community. Obviously it is highly important that unions analyze carefully the results of their wage policies and do not take for granted that every increase in union wage scales is desirable, even from the standpoint of the union members.

Fortunately there is a strong probability that union pressure for higher wages will accelerate technological progress and will stimulate the substitution of indirect methods of production for direct — the use of more chemists, engineers, physicists, and other technicians and of more equipment relative to routine production workers. This assumes, of course, that the technicians are unorganized, or at any rate that their unions are weaker than the unions of the routine production workers. Despite the enormous good which unions are likely to do in accelerating technological progress, it remains true that collective bargaining must be expected to prevent the achievement of the ideal product-mix, to cause a certain amount of wage-distortion unemployment, and perhaps to make the supply price of labor respond so quickly to increases in the demand for labor as to produce a substantial amount of chronic unemployment.

In other words, setting wages by the bargaining power of unions and employers cannot be counted upon to give proper representation to the interest of the community in the highest possible standard of living and in the fair distribution of income. Only by accident and good fortune will the results of collective bargaining be satisfactory. Hence, trade unions, employers, and the community must face the question of whether controls should be developed to guide the process of bargaining.

The first step in the process of control is the development of a body of knowledge concerning the economics of wages — the relationship between wages and productivity, the effect of changes in wage-price relationships upon the volume of employment and the size of the national income, and the possibility of increasing the size of payrolls at the expense of profits. Such knowledge may have only a limited effect upon negotiations in specific cases. Nevertheless, it is a necessary foundation for an informed public opinion both within the trade union movement and in the community at large. Nor should the effect of knowledge upon the outcome of negotiations be underestimated. A conviction that one's position is in the interest of the community as a whole increases the vigor and determination with which one supports that position. Hence, when a union or an employer has the public interest on its side, it supports its case with more than ordinary zeal. On the other hand, a party which has a weak case, according to generally accepted views of the public interest, is likely to be handicapped by knowledge of this fact.

The second step in the control of the process of bargaining is the development of an internal organization capable of representing the interests of labor as a whole. This matter will be discussed in subsequent chapters. Let me call attention here, however, to the fact that the 190-odd national unions are not capable of looking at the interests of labor as a whole; each is too small a part of the whole. The principle of autonomy, which, as I pointed out in the first chapter, has guided the development of the American trade union movement, has prevented either of the two great federations from going far in representing the interests of labor as a whole, especially in cases where the interests of labor as a whole conflict with the interests of particular unions.

The great strength trade unions have acquired makes the well-established principle of autonomy in considerable measure obsolete. Blind driving ahead by individual unions for a higher price of labor can be disastrous for labor as a whole. If the trade union movement were to be successful in developing an organization for representing the interests of labor as a whole, the problem of national wage policy would be largely solved, because organized employees will soon be such a large part of the community that their interests as a group will coincide fairly closely with the interests of the entire community.

Failure of the trade union movement to develop an organization for representing the interests of labor as a whole will probably force intervention by the government. The mildest kind of intervention would be encouragement of a general rise in the price level, a rise sufficient to offset any tendency for unions to push up the price of labor faster than engineers and managers can raise output per man-hour. This might be accomplished by credit policy and by fiscal policy. Such a policy might be sufficient to produce a satisfactory level of employment under collective bargaining. On the other hand, it might not be because it could not prevent developments in the structure of wages which impair the ability of the economy to give employment, such as the development of very high wages in the construction industry which limit the capacity of that industry to provide investment outlets for the community's savings. In fact, the effort of the government to encourage a rise in prices might accentuate the tendency for some prices to advance faster than the general average. Consequently, the government might be compelled to undertake the formidable and hazardous task of enforcing a national wage policy which endeavored to control the wage structure.

Chapter IV

The Government of Trade Unions

I

TRADE UNIONS AIM TO BRING DEMOCRACY AND RESPECT for human rights into industry. Should they themselves be democratic organizations? Are they democratic? Do they show respect for human rights in conducting their own affairs? Is democracy practicable in trade unions? Would democracy mean dissension and division? Would it handicap the unions in dealing with employers? Are the members of trade unions competent to determine policies? If the rank and file had much to say about union policies, would these policies inevitably be based upon inadequate information and fail to produce the results desired by the rank and file? What reforms are needed in the government of trade unions and how may they be achieved?

II

One might say that trade unions should be democratic for the simple reason that the members of *any* organization, whether it be a union or a garden club or a church, ought to control it if they so desire. That is an unsatisfactory way of disposing of the question because it ignores the problems of whether democracy is needed in trade unions and whether it would work in unions.

Democracy is needed in trade unions because there is room for great differences among the members in the objectives of unions, in their policies, and in the ways in which they conduct their affairs. As to objectives, there may be many differences of opinion concerning demands to be made on employers. Should the union press mainly for higher wages or for shorter hours? Should it limit its wage demands in order to get a welfare fund? Should it seek to eliminate piecework or bonus plans? Should it demand that reductions in the demand for labor be met by equal division of work or by dropping the junior men? Should it demand department or plant seniority rules? Should it seek a uniform wage increase for all workers in the plant or the elimination of inequalities? Should it bargain with groups of employers, imposing a uniform rate on each member of the group, or should it make individual bargains with different enterprises, varying the rate of pay in accordance with the ability of the enterprise to pay? Differences over objectives may relate to non-bargaining activities of the union. Should it operate a pension plan or a sick benefit plan or a medical center? Should it provide housing for members? Should it start a bank?

Differences also are likely to exist over policies. How fast should the union attempt to push up wages? How much unemployment should it risk by pressing wage demands? Should the men strike rather than accept a given compromise? Should they strike in sympathy with another union? Should they refuse to handle parts made by a rival union? Should they honor a picket line established by another union?

Finally, conduct of the union's own affairs produces many issues on which the members may differ. Should the union broaden its jurisdiction to admit workers in related industries? Should it limit itself to skilled craftsmen or open its doors to semiskilled specialists? Should it increase its dues in order to build up a defense fund? How far should it go in transferring policymaking from the local unions to the national? How frequently should the union have a convention, and what authority should the convention have to change the constitution of the union? What authority should be given the union president? What reports should the officers make to members? For what offenses should members be disciplined? How should charges against members be tried?

The admission requirements of unions, the offenses for which men may be disciplined, the processes by which charges of violating union rules are tried are important because about seven million workers are employed in either closed shops or union shops and about four million more work under maintenance-of-membership clauses. This means that there are seven million jobs in the United States which can be held only by men who can satisfy the admission requirements of unions and eleven million which can be held only by men who are in good standing in their unions. Plainly the admission requirements of unions and the administration of discipline by unions are affected with a public interest.

III

Before we ask whether democracy in unions is practicable, let us look at the principal facts of trade union government:

1. Admission requirements.
2. The making of union policies.
3. The execution of union policies.
4. Powers of the president.
5. Voting rights of members.
6. Administration of discipline.

1. Admission requirements. In general, unions admit any properly qualified worker without regard to creed, politics, or race and without imposing onerous economic restrictions. And yet restrictions are far from rare. The wire weavers admit only Christians and the railway carmen and the masters, mates, and pilots require belief in a Supreme Being.[1] A substantial number of unions bar Communists and others deny Communists the right to hold office. The United Mine Workers is one of the unions barring membership to Communists. The carpenters' union is another. The A. F. of L. at its 1939 convention advised its constituent unions to exclude Communists.[2] A number of unions still exclude women. Discrimination against Negroes is the most important restriction on union membership. About twenty national unions exclude Negroes either by their constitutions or by their rituals. Many local

---

[1] Joel Seidman, *Union Rights and Union Duties*, p. 37.

[2] *Proceedings of the Fifty-Ninth Annual Convention of the A. F. of L.,* 1939, p. 505.

unions exclude Negroes where the nationals do not. Some unions discriminate against Negroes by putting them in separate locals or by limiting their right to hold office.

A few unions require candidates for admission to serve onerous apprenticeships, but in most cases the terms of apprenticeship are reasonable and experience at the trade is counted as equivalent to apprenticeship. The variation in admission fees is wide. Some nationals limit the fees which their locals may charge. The Amalgamated Clothing Workers puts the limit at $10, the bricklayers at $100, and the lathers at $100. Initiation fees of $200 or more, however, are far from rare, especially in the building trades. The glaziers in Cincinnati charge $400 and in Chicago $1,500. Some locals of the motion picture operators charge $500 to $600. A large local of the teamsters' union in New England, against the advice of its officers, put the initiation fee at $250. Soon the rank and file began to ask that their friends and relatives be taken in for less. As a result, the high fee was repealed. Most restrictive of all is the refusal of a local union to admit anyone. Sometimes the rule is that no one will be admitted while members are out of work. The influence of the national officers of unions is almost invariably against the refusal of locals to accept members. The national officers know that this refusal in the long run will weaken the union by forcing a larger and larger proportion of the workers in the occupation or industry into nonunion shops.

2. The making of trade union policies. The supreme policy-making body in most national unions is the con-

vention which is composed of delegates from local unions. Locals may have votes in proportion to their members, or a limit may be set on the votes given the large locals. The conventions of the Typographical Union, the photo-engravers, the automobile workers, and a few others meet every year. More common is a convention every other year, or every three or four years. During the depression many unions voted to skip the convention. The tobacco workers went thirty-nine years without a convention.[3]

The convention usually has authority to amend the constitution of the union with or without submission of the amendments to a referendum by the rank and file. In a few unions, such as the Typographical Union, national officers are elected by popular vote. In most cases, however, officers are elected by the convention.

Although the convention is the supreme body in the national union, the real government of the union is usually in the hands of the national executive board. There are two principal reasons for this. One is that most policy decisions cannot be held up until the union holds its regular convention. Hence most of them are made by the executive boards and ratified, if that is necessary, by the convention. The second reason is that the executive boards are composed of the men with

---

[3] Among 144 unions (104 A. F. of L. and 40 C.I.O.) the frequency of conventions is as follows: one year, 27; two years, 41; three years, 11; four years, 20; five years, 9; otherwise specified or information not available, 36. The great expense of conventions frequently leads them to be postponed. Among the 40 C.I.O. unions, 12 hold conventions every year and 13 every two years; among 104 A. F. of L. unions, only 15 hold conventions every year and 28 every two years.

the greatest personal influence in the union — full-time officers of the union, the president, vice presidents, and secretary-treasurer. These are the men who administer the policies of the union. The knowledge and power which the officers get as administrators of policies enhances their influence as policy-makers.

3. The execution of union policies. The execution of policies in most unions either is in the hands of the national officers or is supervised by them. The building trades' unions are to a considerable extent an exception to this general rule, partly because competition in this industry is largely local and partly because the local unions are able to take care of themselves. There are many reasons for the ascendancy of national officials, but the principal one is that much of the work of running the trade unions requires skilled personnel and large resources. The national is better able to supply these than the locals. Consider the matter of organizing the unorganized. It is such a difficult job and requires so much money and so much expert personnel that locals do not attempt it except on a small scale.

Most important of all in explaining the growing control of the national unions over the locals are the advantages of requiring national approval of strikes by locals and of centralizing union funds in the hands of the national. In these ways locals are protected from starting hasty and ill-advised strikes which they are almost certain to lose, and the strikes which do occur are more adequately financed. A study of the constitutions of 104 A. F. of L. unions shows that 53 require national approval of strikes before they are legal under the laws of the union and 6 require approval by the national in nearly all cases but permit locals to call strikes without national approval under certain conditions. Of the unions which do not require national approval of strikes, 6 are unions of government employees or teachers which do not expect to use strikes. Among 36 C.I.O. unions studied out of a total of 40 in the federation, 24 require national approval in all cases and 3 more require approval in nearly all cases.

The requirement that locals may strike only with the approval of the national means that the negotiation of agreements falls largely into the hands of nationals. As a matter of fact, local officials are usually glad to shift the responsibility. It is easy for them to be uncompromising and to let national representatives assume the blame for accepting compromises.

Even the administration of trade agreements, especially the handling of important grievances which involve disputes over the meaning of an agreement, is shifting into the hands of nationals. One reason is that the national representatives of the union are better fitted to handle cases than local business agents. National representatives are selected by the presidents of unions, usually from among the more successful local business agents; business agents, on the other hand, are usually elected by the rank and file. The presidents ordinarily select for national representatives better men than the local rank and file pick as business agents. Another reason why the administration of agreements is shifting into the hands of the national unions is that many agreements cover large companies in which there are many locals. In such cases grievances which are appealed to top management or to an umpire are usually handled for the union by a national representative or a district representative.

4. The powers of union presidents. Union presidents do not as a rule have the complete authority over subordinates which corporation presidents possess, but many of them have something close to it, and their power is increasing. The growing responsibility of the national union for organizing the unorganized, for negotiating and administering trade agreements, and for dealing with government agencies means that the union needs a large number of national representatives. Some of the large or moderately large nationals have over 200 organizers or national representatives. In 36 out of 88 A. F. of L. unions, the appointment of national representatives is the exclusive responsibility of the president, in 20 they are appointed by the president with the approval of the executive board, in 3 they are appointed by the executive board. In 29 cases the constitution of the union does not cover the point. Among C.I.O. unions the powers of the president are much more limited. Among 36 C.I.O. unions the appointment of national representatives is the exclusive responsibility of the president in only one, in 21 they are appointed by the president with the approval of the executive board, and in 5 they are appointed by the executive board. In 9 cases the constitution does not cover the point.

It is plain that the right of the president to appoint national representatives gives him enormous political power in the union. This, however, is only a small part of the power now possessed by many union presidents. The following statements are based upon an examination of 88 constitutions of A. F. of L. unions. In 8 national unions the president may remove any international officer, and there is no appeal from his decision. In 13 national unions the president may suspend and revoke the charters of locals without appeal; in 12 national unions the president may discipline and replace local officers without appeal. In a greater number of cases the president may do these things — remove international officers, suspend or revoke local charters, and discipline or supplant local officers — subject to an appeal to the executive board.[4] If the president controls the executive board, as he usually does, this appeal means little. In many unions the executive board may take action from which there is no appeal. For example, in 15 A. F. of L. unions the executive board may remove an international officer (one of its own members) without appeal; in 25 cases it may suspend or revoke local charters; in 11 cases it may discipline and supplant local officers. On the other hand, no one of 36 C.I.O. unions studied gives the president authority to

---

[4] For example, in 20 A. F. of L. unions the president may appoint international representatives with the approval of the executive board; in 12 cases he may remove representatives with the approval of the board; in 20 cases he may suspend or revoke local charters with the approval of the board; in 27 cases he may discipline or supplant local officers with the approval of the board. In 20 C.I.O. unions the president may appoint international representatives with executive board approval; in 3 cases he may suspend or revoke local charters with the approval of the board; and in 4 cases he may discipline or supplant local officers with the approval of the board.

remove international officers without appeal, and only 3 give him authority to discipline or supplant local officers without appeal. In several C.I.O. unions the executive board may take action from which there is no appeal. In 6 unions the executive board may remove an international officer without appeal, in 12 unions it may suspend or revoke charters, in 7 unions it may discipline or supplant local officers.

The authority granted to remove officers or revoke charters is not limited to specific causes. The constitution of the Retail Clerks' International Protective Association permits national officers to suspend locals "for any act of insubordination against the authority of the International." There are no provisions for trial, hearing, or defense. The president of the United Mine Workers, with the approval of the executive council, may remove any international officer "for insubordination or just and sufficient cause."[5] Most sweeping of all is the provision in the by-laws of the American Federation of Musicians which describes the duty and authority of the president thus:

It shall be his duty and prerogative to exercise supervision over the affairs of the Federation; to make decisions in cases where, in his opinion, an emergency exists; and to give effect to such decisions he is authorized and empowered to promulgate and issue executive orders, which shall be conclusive and binding upon all members and/or locals; any such order may by its term (a) enforce the Constitution, By-Laws, Standing Resolutions, or other laws, resolutions or rules of the Federation, or (b) may annul and set aside some or any portion thereof, except such which treat with the finances of the organization

---

[5] Joel Seidman, *Union Rights and Duties*, pp. 26–27.

and substitute therefore other and different provisions of his own making; the power to do so is hereby made absolute in the President when, in his opinion, such orders are necessary to conserve and safeguard the interests of the Federation, the Locals, and/or members.[6]

5. Voting rights of members. Nearly all unions give the same voting rights to all members, except that large locals are sometimes not given representation at the union conventions in proportion to their strength. This is not inequitable as many small locals cannot afford to send delegates. Several unions, however, have recently established Class B membership, which does not have full voting rights. In the carpenters' union, for example, Class B members, who are usually semi-skilled production workers and who do not participate in the union's insurance schemes, have no voting rights in the national convention. In the electrical workers' union (A. F. of L.), locals composed of Class B members have only one vote in the convention.

6. Administration of discipline. Many unions, in order to protect themselves against members who are agents of employers or of outside political groups, permit members to be disciplined for such vague offenses as "slandering an officer," "creating dissension," "undermining the union or working against its interest," "action which is dishonorable or which might injure the labor movement," "circulating written material dealing with trade union business without permission

---

[6] *Constitution, By-Laws, and Standing Resolutions of the American Federation of Musicians,* 1941 edition, Art. 1, Section 1, p. 19.

of the general executive board."[7] When union discipline under these vague and general phrases or similar ones conflicts with the ordinary duties and rights of a citizen, the courts, if appealed to, will give redress, as in the case of a member of one of the railroad brotherhoods who was expelled for signing a petition to the legislature asking reconsideration of a full-crew law,[8] a member of the musicians' union who was expelled for playing in an army band, a member of the plumbers' union who was expelled for using his own judgment instead of following the union's instructions while serving on a plumbing board, or members of various unions who were expelled for testifying truthfully before a court or a commission.

IV

How shall one interpret this picture of the government of trade unions? Are trade unions democratic? If democracy means active participation by the rank and file in policy-making, the answer for most unions is "No." At the local level and on many minor matters there is fairly broad participation by members in

---

[7] Philip Taft, "Judicial Procedure in Labor Unions," *Quarterly Journal of Economics,* May, 1945, pp. 370–385. Examination of the constitutions of 81 unions by Professor Taft showed the several offenses made punishable as follows: slandering an officer, 29 unions; creating dissension, 15 unions; undermining the union or working against its interest, 20 unions; action that is dishonorable or which might injure the labor movement, 25 unions; and circulating written material dealing with union business without permission of the general executive board, 21 unions.

[8] See *Spayd v. Ringing Rock Lodge,* 270 Pa. 67. See John P. Troxell, "Protecting Members' Rights Within the Union," *American Economic Review, Supplement,* March 1942, pp. 460–475.

policy-making. At the national level, policies are made by the professional leaders of the union.

This does not mean the rank and file lack influence. Their influence is great, but influence is not participation. If democracy simply means strong rank and file influence, most unions are democratic. The typical situation in a union is similar to that found in most organizations, churches and clubs of all sorts. There is a minority which is sufficiently interested in the affairs of the organization to attend business meetings and to participate actively in discussing problems. In the case of unions this minority usually asks the officers to press for stiff demands — stiffer than employers would be willing to grant without a long fight, stiff enough to force many employers out of business. In order to avoid trouble, the great majority of the union would settle for much less than the active minority demand.

Quite naturally the professional leader feels on the spot. If he disappoints the active minority too deeply, his leadership will be challenged. If he gets the inactive majority into too much trouble, he may provoke revolt also. He compromises, as, of course, he must. Usually he is more interested in placating the active minority than the inactive majority because he knows that the support or opposition of the active members is more important than the support or opposition of the inactive members. The record shows that union officials lose their jobs, not for being too radical for the majority, but for being too conservative for the minority.

If by democracy is meant active competition for offices, the question as to democracy in unions must be answered by "Yes" and "No." At the local level there is often competition, sometimes on a personal basis and sometimes on a policy basis. For example, a man may run for office on the ground that a younger and more active man is needed, or he may run on a "be tough to management" platform, alleging that the incumbent has learned to see problems too much from management's point of view and that he has grown away from the men in the shop.

At the national level, competition for offices is the exception rather than the rule, especially among the older unions. The International Typographical Union is a striking exception to this rule. Typical of the great majority of national unions are seven studied by Taft.[9] During the period 1910 to 1941, these seven unions held 764 elections to national offices. In 634 elections there was only one candidate. In 63 presidential elections there were nine contests. In three unions (street railwaymen, teamsters, and bricklayers) there were no contests in thirty-one years; in the carmen's union there was only one.

It is not surprising to find that the typical term of service of union presidents is quite long — despite the fact that many men do not reach the presidency until they are at least middle-aged. Daniel Tobin has been president of the teamsters since 1907; George Berry, president of the pressmen since 1908; William L.

---

[9]These unions are the carmen, the street railwaymen, the teamsters, the carpenters, the barbers, the bricklayers, and the hotel and restaurant workers. See Philip Taft, "Opposition to Union Officers in Elections," *Quarterly Journal of Economics*, February, 1944, pp. 246–264.

Hutcheson, president of the carpenters since 1915. Joseph Weber served as president of the musicians for forty years, from 1900 to 1940. Among 89 union presidents who were in office in November, 1946, 23 had served sixteen years or more and 52 had served more than five years.

If one asks whether unions give their members what they want, the proper answer is that for most unions the question is irrelevant. The great majority of the members do not have much opportunity or desire to consider and discuss alternative policies. Hence they are not to be regarded as making a choice. The proper question to ask is: "Do the members like what they get?" The answer to that question is usually "Yes."

V

What changes are needed in trade union government? Let us draw up a few standards which a properly administered trade union government ought to satisfy.

1. Admission requirements. Unions should be open to all qualified persons without regard to race, creed, or political belief. Some people will ask, "Must unions take in Communists?" That depends upon circumstances. Certainly trade unions should be permitted to reject applicants who are believed to be entering the union to change its purposes, in order to convert it from a bargaining agent of workers into the tool of a particular party. In other words, if Republicans, Democrats, or Communists join a union to convert it into a political club, the union is justified in expelling them. On the other hand, the mere fact that a man belongs to

a given party, whether it be Republican, Democratic, or Communist, does not justify a union in excluding him.[10]

2. Voting privileges. All members of the union should have the same right to vote. It is not incompatible with this principle to place reasonable restrictions on the representation given to large locals in conventions or to restrict voting on certain matters to certain members; for example, restricting voting on questions of insurance to the members who are paying for insurance. This principle does preclude dividing members into two classes, such as A and B, with one class having incomplete voting rights.

3. Honesty of elections. The union constitution should contain effective provisions for assuring honest elections. Among other things this means that every candidate should be assured a representative on the board which canvasses the results.

4. Reports to members. Members are entitled to clear and reasonably complete financial statements audited by a certified public accountant.

5. Retirement plan and pensions for officers. It is only fair that unions give to their officers as liberal pensions as they ask that industry give to its employees. Efficient administration would also be promoted by compulsory retirement at the age of 70. The Inter-

---

[10] Obviously a union is justified in excluding a man who is suspected of joining to spy on it for an employer or for another union. Likewise a union is justified in rejecting applicants who have a bad record for union loyalty or who have been expelled from other unions for violating rules, just as employers are justified in refusing to hire men with bad records as employees.

national Ladies' Garment Workers' Union has recently established a retirement fund for its paid officers.[11]

6. *Administration of discipline.* Some discipline for broad and vague offenses probably must be permitted. One does not like to see men tried for such offenses as "creating dissension" or "slandering an officer," but the fact remains that these tactics are regularly used by Communists and •by agents of employers. The charge, however, should be more serious than "creating dissension" or "slandering an officer." Those offenses might be committed on a trivial scale. The only justification for permitting men to be tried for vague offenses is the protection of the life of the union against serious danger. Hence when men are tried for vague offenses, the charge should be "gravely jeopardizing the welfare of the union." Such a charge places a much greater burden of proof upon the accuser than a charge of "creating dissension" or "slandering an officer." Since trial boards are often controlled by the administration, the accused is entitled to have any discipline imposed upon him reviewed for its reasonableness by an outside neutral agency. No union constitution, to my knowledge, makes provision for such review.

7. *Separation of policy-making and policy-executing.* It is unsatisfactory to have policy-making dominated

---

[11]Two-thirds of the cost of the pension fund will be borne by the union and one-third by the officers. Benefits will be paid to male officers retiring at sixty and to women retiring at fifty-five. Pensions will be based on length of service with 2 per cent of normal salary allowed for each year up to a maximum of 50 per cent. Persons who are voted out of office before retirement will receive a full refund of their contributions. About 700 officers are covered by the plan. Benefit payments will begin on January 1, 1949.

by the national officials who are responsible for policy-executing. The national officers, quite properly, regard themselves as more or less permanent officials. Their duties of dealing with employers and government agencies require technical skill and their usefulness increases with experience. And yet when most of the policy-making for the union is done by more or less permanent, full-time officials, the participation of the rank and file in the affairs of the union is severely restricted.

The rank and file are obviously unqualified to decide many matters of union policy, especially matters of wage policy. Furthermore, the union cannot afford to have its unity jeopardized by bitter campaigns in which competition over policies is mixed with competition for offices which carry with them a livelihood. The best solution is to change the composition of the national executive boards of unions from paid officers to men from the shops who serve on a per diem basis, and who make policy with the advice and help of the professional officers. Along with this change should go the adoption of the rule that the professional officers shall serve indefinitely, being subject to removal only for inefficiency or misconduct.

The advice of experienced and well-informed professional officers in matters of policy would probably carry great weight with the nonprofessional executive board. Hence, the formal change in the policy-making machinery would not change the men who really decide questions of policy. Nevertheless, the change would be an important one in two respects. It would improve communication between the rank and file of the union and the professional leaders, a need which is almost as important as the need for better communication within corporations. It would mean that union policies would be changed without changing the full-time and more or less permanent officers of the union. Consequently, it would save members who advocate policy changes from the necessity of attempting to displace the professional officers of the union.

VI

What can be done to bring about the reform of union government? Should action be left to the decision of unions themselves or should the federal government and the states establish certain standards which unions must meet? The government would be wise to move slowly in intervening in union affairs. Three matters, however, involve such fundamental interests that action by the government seems to be called for. They are (1) assuring fair admission requirements; (2) protecting members from unfair discipline by unions; and (3) protecting locals from arbitrarily and unfairly being deprived of self-government.

1. Admission requirements. The prevalence of closed and union shops requires statutes forbidding unions from denying admission to any properly qualified person on the ground of race, creed, or politics. It would be unconstitutional for the government to bar Negroes from running locomotives or from plumbing or carpentry. What would be unconstitutional for the legislature to do should not be permitted by a private organization.

Unions which charge unreasonable initiation fees or which exclude properly qualified persons because of race, creed, or politics should be forbidden to negotiate closed-shop or union-shop contracts and should not be eligible for certification as bargaining agents.

2. Discipline of members. Since eleven million Americans hold their jobs only so long as they are in good standing in unions, the administration of discipline by unions is a matter of public interest. A partial solution is a federal statute applicable to all employers subject to the Wagner Act making it an unfair labor practice for an employer to discharge an employee because of loss of good standing in a union unless the reasonableness of the discharge has been upheld, on appeal by the employee, by the same umpire who passes on discharges by the employer. If the agreement provides for no umpire, the worker might be permitted to appeal to the National Labor Relations Board, just as he might appeal a discharge by the employer for union activity.

Such a statute would protect men from unjust discharge, but not from unjust expulsion from the union. In other words, union officers might still get rid of an inconvenient critic. Since the administration controls the trial machinery in the union or can usually do so if it desires, the only effective protection against arbitrary expulsion is appeal to an outside body. Appeal to courts is too slow and costly. Furthermore, courts usually pass only on the question whether the man had a fair trial, not on whether his offense warranted the penalty. The most appropriate arrangement is appeal to the

National Labor Relations Board on the ground that the complainant is being deprived of union membership for an offense which he did not commit or which does not warrant such an extreme penalty. The work of the National Labor Relations Board and its staff in investigating alleged discriminatory discharges by employers would make the Board an appropriate agency to investigate alleged unjust expulsion by unions. State statutes are needed to protect men who are not covered by the Wagner Act.

3. Protecting local unions from being arbitrarily deprived of self-government. This is another problem which requires a flexible, administrative approach because the seizure may be reasonable or unreasonable, or, if reasonable, it may be unreasonably prolonged. Again the practical remedy seems to be new authority for the National Labor Relations Board. The Board should be authorized to determine whether the members of a local (or the district) are being unfairly and unreasonably deprived of the right to be represented by agents of their own choosing. The offense is analogous to the interference by employers with the self-organization of employees. The National Labor Relations Board is obviously an appropriate body to determine this issue.

Beyond these three steps intervention by the government does not seem to be called for. Government supervision of union elections has been suggested. The task, however, would be enormous, greater by far than is warranted by the problem. Furthermore, supervision of elections by the government could itself be dangerous, leading to too much influence by government in the affairs of unions. Another suggestion is that unions be required to publish financial reports in order to be eligible for certification under the Wagner Act. Important as such reports would be in encouraging more businesslike practices in unions and in discouraging expense account abuses, my vote would be against requiring them. They are not related with sufficient closeness to the rights of members or the process of collective bargaining.

Should the government seek to encourage broader participation by the rank and file in union affairs by requiring that policy-making and policy-executing be separated and by requiring that the responsibility for policy-making between the conventions of unions be vested in nonprofessional executive boards? The answer to this question is obviously "No." Each union must plan the structure of its own government to meet its own conditions and needs. Furthermore, changes of the sort suggested would mean nothing if imposed from the outside.

Is there any likelihood that unions themselves will alter their governments in order to give more participation to nonprofessionals in policy-making? Are not the full-time officers of unions bound to doubt the competency of nonprofessional boards to decide difficult questions of policy? Are they not bound to fear that such boards will get the union into trouble with employers and with other unions? Are they not bound to fear that such boards will be a threat to the influence and prestige of the paid officers?

Many paid officers of unions would undoubtedly oppose the creation of nonprofessional executive boards. Nevertheless, I believe that the proposal would meet with approval from many labor leaders who have devoted their lives to building up trade unions. Most of these men are sincerely devoted to the democratic philosophy. They have fought hard to bring democracy into industry. Many of them are disturbed by the inadequate participation of the rank and file in the affairs of unions, and they are looking for ways of increasing the interest of the members. Nor are most professional leaders likely to believe that nonprofessional executive boards would fail to give careful attention to the recommendations of the professional leaders. They know that the views of the professionals would carry great weight. They know that the conventions which usually have the duty of electing members of the executive board would take this responsibility seriously and would be careful to pick men of experience and mature judgment.

Whether the proposed change in the government of trade unions is regarded favorably or unfavorably by the unions themselves, it is clear that the change must come from within. In fact, the whole problem of developing broader participation in the affairs of unions can be solved only by the unions themselves. All that outside agencies can do is to give some protection to dissenters within unions and to prevent men from being disciplined or expelled because of their views on problems of union policy.

VII

The proposals for the improvement of trade union government which I have outlined will be anathema to some pioneer trade unionists who battled valiantly to build unions before the days of the Wagner Act. These men were brought up to regard unions as private clubs. This conception of trade unions is obsolete. The proposals which I have made are based upon the assumption that unions are quasi-public organizations and that their activities are affected with a public interest. However reluctant you and I may be to abandon the private club conception of unions, acceptance of this new conception of trade unions is inevitable. This new conception of unions springs from the fact that millions of jobs may be held only by men whom trade unions are willing to accept as members. It springs from the fact that additional millions of jobs may be held only by men who are in good standing in unions. It springs from the fact that the government has conferred on unions the exclusive right to bargain for millions of workers — to make bargains which determine the conditions under which these men shall work and the conditions which they must obey or be discharged.

No government would be worthy of the name which gave such tremendous power to private organizations without taking steps to see that the power was exercised in the public interest.

Chapter V

The Problem of Industrial Peace

I

ROUGHLY 12,000 TRADE AGREEMENTS BETWEEN EM-
ployers and unions are said to come up for renewal
each year.[1] If this estimate is correct, the proportion of
agreements settled without strike or lockout in most
prewar years has been roughly four out of five. This
is a good record. During the last year, however, it has
probably not been more than three out of four.[2]

It is important that collective bargaining have a good
record of settling disputes. The economy is highly
interdependent, and is becoming more so. As trade
unionism spreads and as the area of bargaining grows,

---

[1] Precise information on this point is lacking. The estimate is that of
Mr. Ronald W. Houghton, special assistant to the director of the U. S.
Conciliation Service. It is based upon an estimate that there are about
50,000 trade agreements between employers and unions *(New York Times,*
September 11, 1946). I think that the estimate is substantially too low.

[2] The figures compiled by the U. S. Bureau of Labor Statistics are woe-
fully inadequate. These figures should show what proportion of agreements
are renewed without strike year by year. They should show a breakdown
by industries, by national unions, by A. F. of L., C.I.O., and independent
unions, and by duration of the collective bargaining relationship. Until
properly classified data are available, students of industrial relations will
be pretty much in the dark concerning where the incidence of strikes is
highest.

the failure of the two sides to reach agreement means that the community is cut off from a large part or all of the output of essential commodities. When the workers and the employers in an industry ask the community to go without an important commodity or service, such as coal, steel, trucking service, elevator service, steamship service, or railroad service, in order that the union and the employers may test which is willing to stand the longer shutdown, they are asking an extraordinary favor of the public.

Contrary to the impression of many people, the right to shut down an industry in order to force an increase in wages or to prevent such an increase is not a fundamental right; it is a privilege. Among sellers, only employees are permitted to combine to raise the price of their product. Coal miners may combine to raise their wages; but if coal operators combined to raise the price of coal, they would soon be in trouble under the antitrust laws. Only in buying labor are employers permitted to combine for the purpose of keeping down the price which they pay. Meat packers, for example, may combine to keep down the price of labor. Were they to combine to keep down the price of hogs or cattle, they would be in trouble. Both unions and employers, therefore, should exercise great ingenuity and determination to make collective bargaining produce settlements. If it produces strikes or lockouts in important industries very frequently, the community is bound to take away the extraordinary privilege now given trade unions and employers in bargaining over the price of labor and to replace collective bargaining with a different process.

Just how is collective bargaining supposed to work? How does it work? What methods and procedures have been developed to facilitate the process of negotiation and to make negotiations more likely to produce settlements? What can be done to improve the process of collective bargaining and to make it more effective both in averting strikes and lockouts and in building better relations between employers and unions? Are there new approaches to negotiations and new methods of negotiation which promise better results than traditional methods? Can standards of good negotiating practice be drawn up so that conciliators and the public will be able to know whether or not the two sides have made a reasonably conscientious effort to compose their differences before resorting to strikes or lockouts? What are the possibilities and limitations of supplementing negotiation between the parties by conciliation or arbitration? What principles should guide the work of conciliators? When should conciliators intervene and when should they keep out? What are the obligations of trade unions and employers to accept arbitration rather than cut off the community from important or essential commodities or services?

Most of these questions have received little attention. In particular, the community does not realize that there may be good or bad practice in conducting negotiations. Furthermore, the idea has not been developed that both unions and employers have an obligation to the community to adopt the best possible negotiating methods and to make every reasonable effort to reach agreement. Likewise, the idea has not been developed that the two parties have an obligation to give fair consideration to the possibility of arbitration, and not to reject arbitration without good reason. This chapter will explore the conditions which determine the success of collective bargaining in fixing the terms of the labor contract, and the possibilities of making it an even more useful and successful instrument for avoiding strikes and lockouts.

II

Let us first look at the theory or the ideal of collective bargaining. Unfortunately, carefully formulated and comprehensive statements of the theory are virtually nonexistent. Hence, it is necessary to piece together a general theory from isolated statements and from the actual behavior of unions and employers.

The theory of collective bargaining assumes that it is satisfactory to adjust wages and working conditions on the basis of the bargaining power of trade unions and employers. Employees are protected in the right to organize on the ground that they need to combine in order to have roughly the same bargaining power as employers. The bargaining power of each side is determined by several elements, but the most important one by far is the willingness of each side to stand a shutdown rather than to accept certain terms. Hence, the willingness to stand a shutdown is the real force behind the position taken by each side in the negotiations.

What determines whether bargaining produces a settlement or a strike or lockout? This depends upon how accurately each side judges the other's willingness to stand a shutdown. If each side knew accurately the other side's willingness to fight, there would never be a strike or a lockout. Disputes would be settled on the terms which equated the willingness of the two sides to stand a shutdown. The union would know that it could not get more and would not have to accept less. The employer would know that he could not settle for less and would not have to give more.[3] If either side *overestimated* the willingness of the other to fight (while the second side did not underestimate the willingness of the first to fight), there would not be a strike or lockout; rather there would be a *range* of wages or conditions at which each side would prefer to settle rather than to fight. If, however, either side *underestimated* the willingness of the other to fight, a strike or lockout would be inevitable, unless the underestimate by one side was offset by an overestimate by the other side or unless the underestimate was corrected.

Willingness to fight is frequently quite indefinite. Each side may be more or less uncertain concerning the terms which it might accept in order to avoid a fight.

---

[3] For example, in order to force a certain wage increase, say 10 cents an hour, the union members might be willing to strike for eight weeks. Rather than grant the increase, the employer might be willing to shut down for ten weeks. The settlement would not be for so high an increase as 10 cents, because the employer would be willing to stand a longer shutdown to prevent it than the union would be willing to stand to get it. To prevent a smaller increase, say of 5 cents an hour, the employer might be willing to shut down for five weeks, but to get the increase the union might be willing to strike for six weeks. The settlement would not be for as little as 5 cents. Somewhere betwixt and between 5 cents and 10 cents is a figure which equates the willingness of the union and the employer to stand a shutdown. This figure would be the settlement.

Furthermore, willingness to fight is changeable. In fact, it is changing all the time. It depends upon many things: upon what one regards as fair, upon how one thinks given changes in the labor contract will affect one's interest, upon how one happens to feel toward the representative of the other side. Here one sees the importance of negotiations. In the theory of collective bargaining, negotiation is assumed to be a process of mutual education and persuasion. Each side is assumed to enter negotiations with an open mind, ready to hear what the other has to say and to give fair consideration to its evidence and its arguments. In short, negotiation is supposed to be a creative process by which each side learns from the other about its conditions, its needs, and its problems, and seeks to convince the other that its own demands are fair. Negotiation is ordinarily expected to change the minds of each side and to reduce the willingness of each side to fight. It may produce settlements of differences which neither side thought of at the beginning. One of the virtues of negotiating is that the parties direct their arguments at each other rather than at a third party and that the purpose is to produce assent by the other party rather than to win a victory over the other party before a neutral. Thus the process of negotiation itself is supposed to build understanding and good relations.

Collective bargaining in practice differs materially from the model which is assumed in theory. It differs in two ways. At one extreme are negotiations in which neither side remotely considers the possibility of a strike or lockout. The two are on such good terms that each would consider a strike or lockout a calamity. The union is not endeavoring to find the highest wage which the employer would give in order to avoid a strike; the employer is not attempting to find the lowest wage which the union would take in order to avoid a lockout. Each would accept less than it feels entitled to in order to preserve good relations with the other side. Thus the goodwill of the parties toward each other creates a higgling area within which bargaining occurs on the basis of argument and persuasion. The essential nature of the process is to arrive at agreement on changes in wages and conditions which each side regards as fair.

At the other extreme are negotiations in which persuasion takes the form of threats rather than facts and arguments. One side or both may enter negotiations with highly publicized demands and with the firm intention of not being influenced by anything said by the other. Each side may indicate quite plainly that it is not interested in hearing arguments, that the problems of the other do not interest it, that it is entitled to certain changes in conditions, and that, come hell or high water, by blankety blank it is going to get them. Meetings may be devoted to ridiculing each other's demands and arguments, to impugning each other's motives, to endeavoring to impress each other with one's toughness and strength. An able trade union leader recently described collective bargaining as a war of nerves, in which the side wins which keeps its nerve until the last, when the other side caves in. Negotiations which are conducted by parties with closed minds and which take the form of ridicule and threats are not likely to produce settlements. The intervention of conciliators, who help the parties save face and back down from their extreme positions, may be necessary to avert a strike.

III

What are the conditions which affect the quality of negotiations, which determine whether negotiations are primarily an appeal to power or an appeal to justice? They are many. Among the most important are:

1. Day-to-day relations between the union and the employer. Do the parties have a friendly and co-operative relationship which they are interested in preserving and improving or do they have an accumulation of rebuffs, frustrations, insults, grudges, for which they wish to get even? Day-to-day relations determine the answers to these questions. The tone and character of most negotiations are largely set long before the negotiations begin. Not much can be done during the course of the negotiations themselves to change the attitude of the parties toward each other. This is another way of saying that negotiations are only a small part of a larger picture.

Day-to-day relations depend upon many conditions, but most of all upon the willingness of each side to inform itself about the problems of the other and to be interested in the problems of the other. Do representatives of management, for example, have a vivid appreciation of the facts of irregular employment and the problems it makes for the worker? Is management willing to show initiative and enterprise and to take some risks in order to give men steadier work? Do the union rank and file and leaders know the facts about the competition of the employer, about the margins between costs and selling prices, about interindustry competition? In a word, are the workers market-minded? As a rule they are not because they never have had a chance to be.

2. The personality of the negotiators. The wide latitude given representatives of each side in negotiations makes the personality of the negotiators an important determinant of the quality of the negotiations. Some men get to the top in unions and business enterprises because they are vigorous seekers of power, because they are aggressive and determined to have their way and are willing to override obstacles in order to get what they desire. When such men have to handle negotiations, there is little chance that facts or arguments will play much part. Of course, there is always the possibility that two determined and aggressive men may fight each other to a standstill. Hence after several years the quality of negotiations may change. On the other hand, some men get to the top of business concerns and unions partly because they are analytical and reasonable, because they pay attention to facts and are good at appreciating the significance of facts and persuading other people to accept their views of problems and policies. Such men are good at persuading others and are themselves flexible and subject to persuasion. When such men handle cases, negotiations are likely to be successful in averting shutdowns.

3. The nature of the negotiating machinery. Negoti-

ations on behalf of the union may be conducted by local officers or national representatives. Local officers are usually less willing and able to exercise discretion than are national representatives. If a compromise is disapproved by the rank and file, the effect on the political fortunes of a local officer may be quite decisive. If the officer depends upon his job with the union for his livelihood, he may be afraid to accept compromises which are in the interest of the rank and file. This has led a few unions (the bricklayers' union, for example) to forbid business agents from acting as negotiators and to require that negotiations be conducted by a committee made up of members working at the trade. The union believes that such a committee is likely to exercise more independent judgment than paid local officials and is less likely to be influenced by local union politics. National representatives are in most cases willing to exercise greater discretion than local representatives, because they are not dependent for their jobs upon the votes of the local members. The financial responsibility for strikes usually rests upon the national union. In order to protect the national treasury, the national union wishes to settle all possible disputes. A compromise by a national representative which may be unpopular with certain aggressive groups in a local may meet the approval of the rest of the union because it helps to conserve the funds in the national treasury.

In a few cases national representatives are less flexible than local representatives. These are cases in which acceptance of employers' demands would create precedents which might be used against the union in other cases. Consequently, they may refuse to pay much attention to economic facts in some cases. A national representative may be willing to put an employer out of business, thus taking away the jobs of the local members, rather than set a precedent which may embarrass the union in other negotiations.

4. The area of bargaining and the completeness of union organization. When employers negotiate as a group, they are more ready to resist demands which they do not like. A shutdown will affect them all alike. On the other hand, if the union has most of the competitive area pretty well organized, the employers will usually find it possible to pass on most of the higher costs to buyers. Sometimes interindustry competition will prevent this. The net result is that industrial peace is promoted by the organization of negotiations so that all employers in competitive areas are included. In the second chapter I called attention to the fact that employers are representatives of consumers. Negotiations are most likely to produce industrial peace when the area of market organization makes employers weak and ineffective representatives of consumers.

5. Political conditions inside unions — and inside employers' associations, in case employers bargain through an association. Union officers who are fearful of losing their jobs are likely to be messenger boys rather than real negotiators. Indeed, they are only one-way messenger boys, carrying the demands of the union to employers but not the employers' point of view to the union. They dare not be influenced by facts or arguments. They are little interested in understanding

employers' problems. Above all, they are unwilling to attempt to influence the rank and file. It may seem democratic for union officers to be sensitive to the preferences of the rank and file. Obviously, it is not a satisfactory situation, however, for the officers to be timid about communicating unpleasant facts to the rank and file or attempting to give the rank and file the benefit of their advice. Most union officers at the national level are without serious political opposition. This does not necessarily mean, however, that they are leaders. Some of them retain the confidence of the rank and file by keeping their ears to the ground. Such men are not of much value as educators or molders of opinion. The union officer gets criticized from opposite directions. If he is too aggressive and exercises too much influence over the rank and file, he is a threat to democracy. On the other hand, if he is highly sensitive to the preferences of the rank and file, he is a messenger boy rather than a leader. Between these two extremes there is a proper balance.

6. Rivalries between unions or union leaders. In the first chapter I discussed some of the consequences of the breakdown of the principle of exclusive jurisdiction which governed the relations between the unions from the formation of the American Federation of Labor until the formation of the Committee for Industrial Organization. I discussed the effect of the breakdown of this principle upon rivalries between unions and the chaos which has developed in the labor movement. The resulting rivalries between unions are a major obstacle to realism in negotiations. These rivalries make leaders

press demands without regard to the long-run economic consequences to either workers or employers. Negotiations are governed, not by the desire to build up a friendly relationship between the union and the employer, but to win prestige for the union and its leaders in competition with other unions and other leaders.

Rivalries between unions have tended to produce and accentuate rivalries between union leaders. Never has there been so much competition for prestige. Who will be the first to set the pattern of wage increases; who will get the largest wage increase? Considerations such as these have governed the conduct of negotiations. In the automobile industry, in the steel industry, in the railroad industry, industrial relations during the last year have been greatly affected by personal rivalries.

7. Knowledge of the facts of American industry, and knowledge or lack of knowledge of the economic implications of various arguments used in wage negotiations. Facts and knowledge are enemies of emotion and of extravagant claims and arguments. Facts do not eliminate emotion; they do not prevent bickering and name calling, but they at least lessen the possible points of disagreement. For example, assume that the employers are resisting a wage demand on the ground that non-union competitors have been making large inroads on the union part of the business, a common situation and a common argument. In some industries, such as hosiery, fairly complete facts are available. The number of new knitting machines going into the industry each year is known and whether the machines have gone into

union or nonunion mills. There is room to argue over the interpretation of the facts, but not over what are the facts.

Both employers and union representatives, as a rule, argue about proposed wage changes with little knowledge of the general economic implications of the arguments which they use. It is interesting to speculate whether the demands of either unions or employers and the arguments used by them in support of their positions would be materially altered if both sides were well aware of the economic implications of certain arguments. Consider four arguments:

1. Changes in the cost of living as the basis for wage increases or decreases.

2. The argument that wages in an industry should not be raised because productivity has not gone up or that they should be raised because productivity has gone up.

3. The argument that a rise in wages would increase employment by raising consumer purchasing power.

4. The argument that wages in one place should be reduced or increased in order to make them uniform with wages in another place.

If the limitations of these arguments were understood, they would be used much more sparingly because the opposing side would point out these limitations. Unions would base wage demands largely upon the argument that workers in the occupation, industry, or place are underpaid in relation to wages received by men of similar skill and responsibility elsewhere or that wage increases were needed to attract more men into the industry, occupation, or place. Extravagant and extreme wage demands would be discouraged, much of the emotion would be taken out of wage negotiations, and the proceedings would be on a saner basis.

IV

Collective bargaining, in order to flourish, must command respect; in order to command respect, it must be more than a mere attempt to settle wages on the basis of bargaining power. It must not be a war of nerves, a competition in toughness, a process of mutual threatening. Nor must it be a contest in stubbornness in which people with closed minds test which side is willing to spend more weeks in negotiation. If collective bargaining is to command respect, it must be an attempt to determine what is fair. This means that it must be guided by criteria of what wages and conditions are fair, that it must be a careful exploration of the facts in the particular situation, and especially of the problems of each side. Negotiations must be conducted by men of goodwill, who have open minds, who appeal to reason, and who are willing to listen to appeals to reason. These are stiff conditions, but neither employers nor unions can expect the community to set much value upon a process which attempts to fix wages and working conditions merely on the basis of the relative willingness of the two sides to engage in a fight.

What can be done to make collective bargaining meet these standards? The steps may be divided into general steps which affect the situation in which negotiations occur and specific steps by which the parties themselves may improve the negotiating process.

Three principal general steps would be helpful. Most basic of all is building up a body of thought on what constitutes a fair structure of wages and what constitute fair changes in wages as conditions change. Obviously such a body of thought cannot be created overnight. The literature of economics contains much on the subject, but many problems remain to be explored. Whatever body of thought exists on these issues needs constantly to be re-examined and revised in the light of the advance of economics. A second general step for improving collective bargaining is building a friendly day-to-day relationship between the union and the management, a problem which I discussed briefly in the second chapter. There is no substitute for good day-to-day relations. Unless they exist, negotiations will be more or less at arm's length. A third general step in improving collective bargaining is the discouragement of competition between unions and between union leaders. An important aid in discouraging this competition is the development of public policies which limit the right of unions to use strikes and boycotts for the purpose of compelling workers to shift from one union to another.

What specific steps can the parties themselves take to improve the process of collective bargaining?

1. Begin the process of negotiations with *proposals,* not demands. Demands imply closed minds, firmly held conclusions. Some unions are careful to avoid the word "demand." If the process of negotiation is to be an appeal to reason, each side must enter the conference with a real expectation of being influenced by the argu-

ments and the evidence which the other side offers.

2. Avoid taking public positions for or against certain proposals in advance of negotiations. It is a mistake for the employer to announce that he will "never" concede this, or for the union to announce that it "must" gain a certain change in the contract, and that it will not consider anything less. Publicly announced "nevers" and "musts" are likely to plague the party responsible.

3. Avoid taking strike votes before the process of negotiation begins. Each side should regard a strike or a lockout as a remote possibility, to be started only as a last resort after ingenuity and patience have failed to find an alternative. A strike vote in advance of hearing the arguments of the other side is inconsistent with an attempt to settle differences on the basis of an appeal to what is fair.

4. Give negotiators proper authority to bargain. Sometimes the two sides bind their representatives too closely by instructions not to concede this or that. Sometimes they give their representatives authority to say "No," but not authority to say "Yes." Both unions and employers are guilty of unduly restricting the authority of their negotiators. It is often necessary for the union to provide that the terms agreed to by its representatives will be submitted for ratification to the rank and file. The representatives, however, should not be unduly restricted in the terms which they are authorized to accept.

Sometimes the process of negotiation is impaired unduly because national unions or multiple-plant companies have uniform national policies which their negotiators are not permitted to alter. Some uniform national policies are necessary. The number of such policies, however, has been growing rapidly and is probably too large. Many unions, for example, now cover several industries. A policy which is appropriate in one industry is not necessarily appropriate in another.

5. Avoid unnecessary delays in beginning negotiations and in conducting them. Deliberate stalling by one side or the other gives rise to antagonisms. Both employers and unions are guilty of stalling. If delay is necessary, let the side which needs it ask for it and state its reasons.

6. Insist on offering facts and arguments. Welcome facts and arguments which are presented by the other side. Sponsor collection of facts by neutral agencies for the use of both sides. Concede agreement with facts and arguments regardless of whether this agreement carries agreement concerning conclusions. It is interesting to speculate how far one side, by insisting on facts and arguments, can compel the other side to offer facts and arguments in return and to make negotiations a discussion of mutual problems rather than a series of recriminations and threats. Certainly not in all cases will a matter-of-fact approach by one side be effective in influencing the other side. In some cases, however, the entire basis of discussion may be altered.

7. Make plenty of proposals. The more proposals each side makes, the greater are the opportunities to find compromises. Unions usually offer plenty of proposals, but many employers have been delinquent in

making them. Indeed, many employers have assumed that proposals should come from the unions and have contented themselves by simply saying "No." The members of the union, however, are likely to measure the outcome of negotiations by the disposition of certain key proposals. The more proposals employers make, the greater is the opportunity to grant key proposals of the union on terms which are acceptable to employers.

Some unions and some employers maintain a list of changes in the contract which they would like to bring about. Such a list, if it is the result of discussions with the employees or with the supervisors who work under the contract, will be quite lengthy — far longer than could be considered in any single negotiation.

8. Be prepared to compromise. This means that each side should propose more changes than it expects to get. There has been much dispute over whether it is better for employers and unions to ask only what they are willing to fight for, or whether each side should propose considerably more than it would be willing, if necessary, to accept. If each side quite definitely regards its proposals as the minimum terms which it is willing to accept, this is in reality the equivalent of entering the conference with a closed mind. If negotiations are to be a process of exploring the problems of each side and of working out fair compromises, both unions and employers should suggest more than they might be willing to accept. This, of course, does not mean that their proposals should be extravagant or unrealistic. The proposals should be carefully considered before being

offered and they should have real merit.

9. Be prepared to get results gradually. One reason for the success of collective bargaining in the stove foundry industry is that each side has taken the trouble to give the other side an opportunity to prepare constituents to accept changes. For example, when employers many years ago wished changes in the union apprentice ratio, they did not expect a concession the first year that the matter was brought up. They gave the union officers a chance to take up the matter with the rank and file and to inform the rank and file about the merits in the employers' case. Of course, this presupposes leaders on each side who are willing to go back to their constituents with facts and arguments presented by the other side and to present honestly and clearly the point of view of the other party.

10. Preserve good manners and keep discussion focused on relevant issues. This prevents the will to settle from being impaired by insults and threats. How is it to be done? A chairman of the conference can do it if he wishes, but it is desirable for both sides to fortify him with clear and definite instructions on this point. In Sweden and England the two parties frequently invite a representative of the Conciliation Service or some other neutral to preside over the negotiations. His duty is not to conciliate — simply to preserve good manners and to keep discussion to the point. It is a good procedure because the neutral is a symbol of the importance of decorum in negotiations — of the fact that the ranting, roaring, table-pounding representative belongs to the barbaric past.

11. Be prepared to stand a long and hard strike or lockout (as the case may be) in order to force a settlement justified by facts and arguments. If one side finds that threats work, it will use them, just as a baby will boss its parents by crying if it finds that crying works. If one side is determined to be truculent, to scorn facts and arguments, and to dictate the terms of settlement, the only way to change the character of negotiations and to show that toughness does not pay is for the other side to back its preference for facts and arguments by forcing a showdown. After a tough negotiator has learned by experience the cost of a shutdown, he may be willing the next time to help discover a basis for compromise.

Let me conclude this discussion of the possibility of improving the procedures of negotiation by asking whether negotiations can continue to be informative and creative after the two sides have been dealing with each other for many years. Does not their knowledge of each other's problems become so complete that there is little for negotiation to do?

Employers and leaders of unions of whom I have asked that question tell me that the answer is "No." The representatives of both sides change. As a rule, the turnover is not a rapid one. Nevertheless, it means that the process of getting acquainted and keeping acquainted is a continuous one. Acquaintanceship is not accomplished once and for all. Furthermore, and perhaps more important, new problems are constantly arising. In the railroad industry it may be problems associated with the introduction of Diesel locomotives, with the steadily increasing speed and length of trains, or with the radical changes which in recent years have been introduced into the maintenance of track. In the metal trades it may be problems introduced as a result of the extensive use of welding. Prefabricated housing, not to mention many new materials, create problems in building. In hosiery the use of nylon and the introduction of new types of machines create problems. New machines and competition from substitutes create problems in coal. Geographical shifts in many industries produce problems for unions and employers. Interindustry competition is steadily growing in importance and frequently produces new problems: the competition of trucks, buses, and airplanes with railroads; competition of aluminum with steel; competition of welding and forging with molding; competition of buses and private automobiles with street railways.

V

The process of negotiation, however much perfected, cannot be counted upon *always* to produce settlements. What should happen when the parties are unable to reach agreement?

Sometimes negotiators, who are not able to reach agreement when left to themselves, are able to do so when assisted by conciliators. Hence, the government should have a strong, competent, and respected conciliation service. How can the conciliation service be made strong, competent, and respected, and how and when should conciliators intervene?

The effectiveness of a conciliation service depends in large measure upon its reputation for impartiality. Effective conciliators must usually have had practical experience in handling labor disputes as negotiators either for employers or for trade unions. The fact that a conciliator was once a union representative or the industrial relations manager of a plant does not mean that he is not capable of being fair. There are plenty of fair-minded men in the service of unions and in the service of business concerns. Some large employers prefer that conciliators shall have had a labor background. Such men are usually able to deal more effectively with union negotiators than conciliators who have never been in the service of unions. In order to create confidence, the conciliation service should operate under the direction of a joint committee composed equally of union representatives and of employer representatives. The joint labor-employer committee should keep in close touch with the operations of the conciliation service. It should meet at least quarterly to receive reports from the director of the service and to review the operations of the service. No person should be appointed to the staff of conciliators without first being approved by both labor and employer representatives.

When should conciliators intervene? It is important to realize that conciliation may do harm as well as good, and that there may be too much conciliation. The mere fact that the employer and the union have been having a difficult time in reaching agreement does not mean that conciliation is indicated. The need for the help of conciliators may be a symptom of bad negotiating procedure, especially if the parties have got themselves into a position where faces need to be saved. Furthermore, if the parties are able easily to shift to conciliators, the responsibility for bringing about a compromise or conciliation (or the prospect of it) may interfere with the bargaining process itself. If the parties can always rely upon the conciliator to extricate them from difficult or extreme conditions, they will not offer to make compromises. In other words, a conciliation service which interferes too frequently and too realistically actually encourages the parties to be unrealistic and uncompromising. Cool indifference by the government to the difficulties of the parties will often have a wholesome effect upon bargaining. Indeed, the experience of a long and tough struggle may be necessary to bring about realism in negotiations and a frank facing of facts. All of this means that the conciliation service must exercise its judgment as to whether to attempt to intervene or to let the strike occur.

What should conciliators do? One of their principal uses has been to help each side take a more realistic view of the other side's willingness to fight. I pointed out early in this chapter that an underestimate by one side of the other's willingness to fight will produce a strike or lockout — unless offset by a compensating overestimate. If the negotiations have involved much bluffing by each side, the help of the conciliator may be needed to find a basis for settlement. Perhaps the most common service performed by a conciliator is "saving faces." Each side is likely to attempt to impress the other side by the device of being tough and un-yielding. Having tried this tactic, each side is likely to fear that willingness to compromise will be interpreted as weakness and will be met, not by a reciprocal will-ingness of the other side to make concessions, but by a stiffening of the attitude of the other side. "Saving faces" is undoubtedly a useful way of preventing strikes and lockouts. Nevertheless, it is a dangerous procedure and one which is easily overdone. Certainly it tends to retard the development of good negotiating procedure. The interests of good industrial relations in the long run are often best served by forcing the two sides to take the consequences of their intransigence. Certainly if they are forced into a strike or a lockout as a result of bad negotiating procedure, next time they will be more careful to avoid getting themselves out on a limb. Consequently conciliators should not help the two sides save face without requiring that each side assume a fairly substantial measure of responsibility for sponsor-ing a compromise. If bad negotiators are saved by con-ciliators from getting their constituents into trouble, the constituents are likely to be slow in replacing the bad negotiators with good ones.

VI

If conciliation fails, it is standard practice for the conciliators to urge arbitration. This is all to the good. Both trade unions and employers, however, have been quite casual in refusing to go to arbitration. The pro-priety of either side in refusing arbitration needs to be reconsidered by trade unions, employers, and the general public. When either party refuses arbitration, it is virtually taking the position that the right of the two sides to engage in a fight over differences which may be quite small is superior to the claim of the public for an uninterrupted supply of goods. Only in very rare and unusual cases is the right of the parties to fight it out superior to the claims of the public.

It has been suggested that the union and the employer before engaging in a strike or lockout issue a joint statement to the public stating just what the fight is about — that is, just how far apart the two sides are in the terms which each is willing to accept. If one side or both have rejected arbitration, the statement might contain an explanation of just why arbitration was unacceptable. This practice could not be easily imposed by law and it could not be followed rigidly. Under some circumstances the expectation that each side might be compelled to make public its offers might impede the process of bargaining. The firm or the union might fear that, if the case went to arbitration, disclosure of offers would be used against it. Nevertheless, the idea is fundamentally sound that strikes or lockouts should not occur unless the two sides are willing to say rather precisely what the unsettled issues are and how far apart the negotiations have left the parties.

One of the most important obstacles in getting the parties to accept arbitration is the difficulty in agreeing on arbitrators. The conciliation service now maintains a list of arbitrators in all sections of the country who have been approved for impartiality and competence by both employer and labor members of the joint advisory committee of the Conciliation Service. The existence of this panel should enormously simplify the selection of arbitrators. Each side can be given the opportunity to pick one man from the panel. To these two may be given the difficult problem of picking the third arbitrator. Since the first two are presumably impartial to begin with, they should be able to pick a third without extreme difficulty.

Suppose that arbitration is rejected. A proposal frequently made during the last several years is that the government appoint a so-called "fact-finding" board. Provision for such boards is made in the Railway Labor Act. In that act, however, they are called "emergency" boards rather than "fact-finding" boards. The British law provides for the appointment of special courts of inquiry. The term "fact-finding" is extremely unfortunate. It implies that the duty of the board is to find the significant facts and report them to the public. Merely finding facts, however, is not very helpful. The public is interested in recommendations. All of the so-called fact-finding boards appointed during the last year have made recommendations. When they assume this responsibility, the recommendations necessarily become far more important than the findings of fact, and "fact-finding" becomes a misnomer for the board. Hence, the term "fact-finding" should be carefully avoided. Emergency boards or boards of inquiry are much better terms.

The practice of appointing emergency boards is open to serious objections. Certainly emergency boards should be appointed very sparingly. If the two sides can *count* on the appointment of a board, the process of bargaining is likely to be impeded. Furthermore, the emergency board has serious defects which limit its usefulness. For example, it differs from a board of arbitration in not having specific points of dispute referred to it for adjudication. Part of its job is to define the differences between the parties. Any board of arbitration which undertook to arbitrate without having before it an agreed statement of issues in dispute would be grievously handicapped. This handicap is not removed by calling a board an emergency board or a board of inquiry. In the second place, in the case of arbitration the parties have the opportunity to select members of the board. This they do not have in the case of emergency boards or boards of inquiry. Finally, in the case of arbitration the parties bind themselves to accept the award. They do not bind themselves to accept recommendations of an emergency board. Hence, the recommendations simply become another step in the process, the basis for further bargaining. Until the board has rendered its decision, both sides hold out. Most fundamental of all is the question of whether the government should appoint an emergency board or insist that the parties withdraw their rejection of arbitration. If the dispute threatens the public health and public welfare so seriously as to justify the appointment of an emergency board, does it not justify putting extreme pressure on the parties to accept arbitration? Certainly one of the issues which emergency boards might well investigate is whether the differences between the parties are sufficiently great to justify their interrupting the production of important or essential commodities or services. Another matter which the emergency boards might well investigate is whether the parties are justified in rejecting arbitration. Up to now, emergency boards have not made investigations of these types; rather they have studied the merits of the dispute itself. A step forward in the technique of using emergency boards would be taken if emergency boards were to focus attention upon these last two questions.

VII

What may the country look forward to? Is the process of negotiating agreements likely to change? Is it likely to continue to be in many cases a process of bellowing and ranting or of sullen refusal to consider evidence? Is it likely to be based upon an appeal to principles, upon a careful collection of facts, upon arguments which are not clever sophistries but which are intellectually respectable? I am optimistic. The next decade, I am confident, will see a revolution in methods of negotiating. Indeed, ten years from now the country will regard the negotiating methods of 1946 as unbelievably crude and primitive.

One must not expect, however, that collective bargaining, though much perfected, will prevent *all* strikes. Indeed, it is an essential part of the theory of collective bargaining that the freedom of the two sides to settle their disputes by fighting is more important than the interest of the public in continuous service. Hence the areas in which collective bargaining may be appropriately relied upon to fix the terms of employment are those in which the public's need for continuous service is regarded as less important than the freedom of the parties to fight each other. Undoubtedly freedom of the parties to fight is important, though its importance varies with the issue in dispute. The need of the public for continuous service varies, of course, with different industries. Should the freedom of the parties to fight each other take precedence in *all* industries over the need of the parties for continuous service? Are there *some* industries in which the need for continuous service is more important than the freedom of the parties to fight? If so, where should the line be drawn between the industries in which freedom to fight is paramount and those in which need for continuous service is paramount? And if a line is drawn, how shall the interest of the public in continuous service be safeguarded? These matters, among others, will be considered in the next chapter.

Chapter VI

Trade Unions

and the Public Interest

I

THE LABOR MOVEMENT WHICH HAS DEVELOPED IN THE
United States during the last fifteen years is, as I have
pointed out, the largest, the most powerful, and the
most aggressive that the world has ever seen; and the
strongest unions, as I have also pointed out, are the
most powerful private economic organizations in the
country. Such organizations are obviously bound to be
a great influence either for good or for harm. What
does the community propose to do both to control the
power of unions and also to help them develop their
enormous constructive possibilities?

The theory of collective bargaining assumes that the
power of unions will be more or less roughly offset by
the power of employers. Hence it is assumed that setting wages and working conditions on the basis of
bargaining power will usually result in equity. This
may seem like a reckless assumption. Nevertheless, in
most cases the assumption of the theory corresponds to
reality. This greatly reduces the necessity of intervention by the government in industrial relations. It does

not, however, eliminate the necessity. In some cases employers may not be strong enough to be a match for unions. In other cases they may be willing to accept the demands of unions and to pass on the cost to the public. In a few cases, equality of bargaining power may actually aggravate the problem of protecting the public interest. When the parties are more or less equal in strength, strikes and lockouts, if they come, are likely to be of long duration. This may not be of great public concern in most industries. In industries which produce essential services, however, the very fact that a long shutdown may be required to determine which side is the stronger increases the difficulty of safeguarding the public interest.

To some extent, the problem of protecting the public interest from harmful actions of trade unions has been examined in previous chapters. In the second chapter I discussed the problem of preventing unions from enforcing working rules which reduce the standard of living of the community; in the third chapter, the problem of preventing union wage policies from having unfavorable effects upon the standard of living. In the third chapter I examined also the problem of preventing unions from unreasonably restricting the opportunity of men to enter given trades or industries or to keep their jobs in given trades or industries.

There are other problems created by the great power of unions which I have not discussed. In a few cases unions have refused to negotiate with employers, but have adopted the practice of unilaterally imposing certain conditions upon employers by union rule. Some unions have not limited their activities to bargaining over the terms of employment for their members. They have used their bargaining power or have attempted to use it (a) to compel employers to violate the law; (b) to force changes in public policy; or (c) to compel union members to shift from one union to another or to punish them for joining the "wrong" union. Finally, there is the problem of protecting the community from strikes which jeopardize the public health or public safety or which deprive the public of essential services. Such strikes have been far from uncommon during the last year. In the fall of 1945, New York had an elevator strike which paralyzed a large part of the industry of the city; in February, 1946, it had a tugmen's strike which threw hundreds of thousands out of work; in September, 1946, it had a truckers' strike which halted the distribution of food and threatened to produce a fuel crisis. In the summer of 1946, Milwaukee had its gas shut off; in the fall of 1946, Pittsburgh had a power strike which threw 100,000 persons out of work for the greater part of a month. In the winter of 1946, the country had its steel production cut off; in the spring, its coal production and its railroad service; and in the fall, its coal production was again shut off. What can and should the community do to protect itself against strikes in essential industries?

II

Let us examine briefly the several problems created by the great power of unions, and then let us explore the possibilities of developing the enormous constructive possibilities of unions.

A number of unions, of which the International Typographical Union is the principal one, have adopted the practice of forcing certain changes upon employers without going through the process of negotiating with them. The unions do this by the simple process of amending their constitutions or by-laws and insisting that, after the expiration of present contracts, members conduct themselves in accordance with the new rules. This practice is obviously wrong and, if generally adopted by unions, would destroy collective bargaining. It means that employers have no chance to influence union opinion by fact or argument. If employers were to adopt the practice, they would be hailed before the National Labor Relations Board, charged with refusal to bargain in good faith, an unfair labor practice. The Board would, without question, hold against employers on this issue.

What is not permitted to employers should not be allowed to unions. What should be done? Some people suggest that the Wagner Act be amended so as to make the obligation to bargain in good faith apply to unions as well as to employers. Others suggest that the section of the Act requiring employers to bargain in good faith be repealed. Either change would equalize the duties of employers and unions and would be an improvement over the present one-sided law. It is a close question which change is preferable. In favor of repeal is the prospect that a requirement that unions bargain in good faith would probably have little effect in the case of strong unions. Nevertheless, the requirement, if properly enforced, would halt the tendency for a few unions to put rules governing working conditions in their constitutions and bylaws. In any event the obligation to bargain in good faith should not be applied to employers unless it is also applied to unions.

III

What should the community do about strikes to compel violations of the law, to compel changes in public policy, to force trade unionists to shift their union affiliation, or to punish them for joining the "wrong" union? Is it sound public policy to take away the right to strike for any of these three purposes?

On few questions of the day is thinking more muddled and confused than on the much-discussed "right" of workers to strike. Some trade union leaders confuse the right to strike with the right to quit. This leads them, as I have pointed out, to conclude that *any* limitations on the right to strike are incompatible with free labor and with democracy itself. Typical of the viewpoint of labor are the following statements recently made by President Green of the American Federation of Labor and Mr. Joseph Padway, general counsel of the Federation. Testifying before a subcommittee of the House Labor Committee in July, 1946, Mr. Green said:

The strike cannot be made illegal without subjecting workers to involuntary servitude.

Writing in the *American Federationist* in July, 1946, Mr. Green said:

The right to strike distinguishes the free worker from the

[158]

slave. The right to strike involves the foundation of our free economy. . . .

Mr. Padway, writing in the *American Federationist* in January, 1946, said:

No extensive discussion is necessary to show that any peacetime prohibition on the right to strike, no matter how limited in time, directly assaults the very props of our democratic structure and violates the constitutional prescription against the imposition of involuntary servitude. . . .

The positions of Mr. Green and Mr. Padway are untenable. They concede no rights to the community. They amount to a claim that the right to strike is superior to all other rights and that, wherever a conflict occurs between the right to strike and other rights, the right to strike shall prevail. This would obviously be ridiculous. It would leave any group of workers free to use its economic power to dictate terms to the community on any subject. Surely there are certain types of strikes which should not be legal. Among them are strikes to compel employers to violate the law, strikes to coerce the government, strikes to deprive workers of the right to belong to unions of their own choosing, or to punish them for belonging to the "wrong" union.

Strikes to compel employers to violate a law require no discussion. They are obviously illegal. Mr. Green and Mr. Padway would probably not defend them. Strangely enough, the law which unions most commonly seek to compel employers to violate is the Wagner Act. This occurs when a union which has not been certified as the bargaining agent strikes to compel the employer to deal with it instead of the union duly certified by the National Labor Relations Board. Mr. Green has called the Wagner Act labor's "Magna Charta." Would he regard it as transforming free workers into slaves if workers are not permitted to strike for the purpose of compelling employers to disregard labor's "Magna Charta?"

Strikes designed to coerce the government should plainly be illegal because they are serious attacks upon free institutions. In the spring of 1946, a strike of the New York subway workers was threatened in the event that the city sold a power plant to a private purchaser. In the Pittsburgh power strike in September, 1946, a temporary injunction against a work stoppage was dissolved after the strikers had voted 4 to 1 against considering a company offer until the injunction was dissolved. The seamen's strike in September, 1946, was an attempt to force a change in the government's wage policy and was successful.

The fact that workers have an important grievance against the government does not justify their striking to force changes in public policy. Every economic group from time to time has grievances against the government. Certainly if labor is permitted to strike to force changes in public policy, bankers, insurance companies, manufacturers, farmers, and all other economic groups should have the equivalent right — that is, the right to combine for the purpose of putting economic pressure on the government. One need not ask what would happen to free institutions if all groups in the community undertook to use economic coercion to force changes in public policy.

Strikes and boycotts for the purpose of compelling workers to shift from one union to another or to punish them for belonging to the "wrong" union should also be made illegal. Such strikes and boycotts have been increasing rapidly in number during the last few years. They are a manifestation of the breakdown of the principle of exclusive jurisdiction upon which the trade union movement operated from 1886 until the middle thirties, of the growing rivalry between unions, and of the diminishing respect for long-established jurisdictional lines. A principle of the Wagner Act is that workers are entitled to be represented by unions of their own choosing. Is not this sound? If it is, should not the voluntary principle be protected from interference regardless of whether the interference comes from employers or from other unions? Would free workers be converted into slaves if they were protected from strikes intended to compel them to shift their union affiliation against their will?

Control of the use of strikes and boycotts by some unions against other unions is needed, not only to protect the rights of individual workers, but in order to protect the trade union movement against interunion warfare and to protect the interest of the community in efficient industry. Interunion warfare is likely to grow in a cumulative manner, as one union retaliates for the attacks of another. The teamsters' union is already well advanced in its program to compel certain classes of workers to leave the brewery workers' union and to join the teamsters' union. The teamsters' union accomplishes its purpose by the simple process of refusing to service breweries where the workers in dispute are members of the brewery workers' union. In many cities A. F. of L. building trades' locals refuse to handle C.I.O.-made building materials. The day may come when the United Automobile Workers will imitate the methods of the A. F. of L. building trades' unions by refusing to handle automobile parts which are made by A. F. of L. workers. Carried to its logical extreme, unrestrained warfare between unions over the affiliation of workers would divide the American economy into two parts — one a C.I.O. part, consisting only of firms which dealt as buyers and sellers with other firms which employ C. I.O. workers, and the second an A. F. of L. part, consisting only of firms which dealt as buyers and sellers with firms employing A. F. of L. workers! Obviously the community cannot permit the efficiency of industry to be impaired by this sort of development. It is a sound principle that the privilege of striking has been given workers for the purpose of helping them to bargain with employers, not for the purpose of permitting them to control the union affiliation of other workers.

IV

What would be the practical effect of depriving men of the right to strike for the purpose of compelling violations of law, of coercing the government, or of forcing other workers to change their union affiliations? Would it prevent all strikes for these purposes? Would it reduce the number of such strikes? What would happen to men who struck to achieve an illegal purpose?

Certainly depriving men of the right to strike for given purposes would not prevent all such strikes. It would, however, virtually assure that strikes for an illegal purpose would fail to accomplish their objectives. This would be the most important result of making strikes for certain purposes illegal. In addition, the fact that strikes for these purposes would be virtually certain to fail would diminish their number.

What would happen to men who engaged in an illegal strike? Many people assume that the strikers would be sent to jail, or at least be fined. Strikes for certain purposes might, of course, be made criminal offenses. This, however, is unnecessary and, in my judgment, would as a general rule be unwise. Nor would depriving men of the right to strike mean that they were compelled to continue working. They have the constitutional right to quit, and they cannot be deprived of it. Depriving men of the right to strike for certain purposes would simply mean that when men quit for those purposes, they would terminate their employment. In other words, men would be deprived of the right to retain their status as employees while abstaining from work in order to accomplish certain illegal results. That is the essential meaning of depriving men of the right to strike.

The strikers, if permitted to do so, would attempt to bargain with the employer to be taken back, not as new employees, but with no impairment of rights (such as seniority rights, vacation rights, group insurance rights, pension rights) which depend upon length of service. Were the men able to make such a bargain, they would obviously defeat the program of depriving them of the right to strike for certain illegal purposes. Hence, in order effectively to implement the program, the employer should be prohibited from rehiring any of the strikers except as new employees, with the seniority rights, vacation rights, insurance rights, and pension rights of new employees. In addition, the employer should be specifically authorized to refuse re-employment to men who engage in an illegal strike if he so desires, and he should be prohibited from dismissing any man hired during the strike in order to rehire one of the strikers. Finally, all picketing in support of illegal strikes should be prohibited and penalized and all other activities in support of illegal strikes, such as paying strike benefits or holding strike meetings, should be penalized. Although the above program would not prevent all illegal strikes, it would make striking for an illegal purpose quite unattractive. Furthermore, as I have pointed out, it would virtually assure that the attempt to accomplish an illegal purpose by striking would fail.

V

What about strikes or lockouts which gravely jeopardize the public health, the public safety, or the general welfare? The general rule which the community has been following up to now is that the freedom of employers and unions to fight each other through strikes and lockouts is more important than the need of the public for continuous service. Is this true of *all* industries? Are there not *some* industries in which the need for continuous service is more important than the freedom of the parties to fight? I submit that in the following three categories the need for continuous service is more important than the freedom of the parties to fight:

1. Hospitals and institutions.
2. Railway transportation.
3. Production of electricity for light and power.

It is not necessary for me to develop the reasons for putting continuous service in these industries above the freedom of the two sides to fight. You can visualize what a calamity would be caused by a strike of nurses in a hospital. A stoppage of train service for two or three days such as occurred last spring would not be disastrous, but what of a stoppage of four weeks, which was the duration of the steel strike in the winter of 1946, or one of over 100 days, which was the duration of the General Motors strike? Consider what a shutdown of electric light and power would mean in a large city in midwinter. Thousands of houses, many of them belonging to union members or business agents, would be cold, because oil burners do not run without electricity. Many factories and stores which depend for their operation upon electricity would close. Elevators would not run, and unless transportation systems had their own source of power, street cars and subways would not operate. A nation-wide stoppage in the coal industry or the steel industry would also soon become a national disaster.

The government should have adequate authority

and well-planned policies to protect the community against strikes or lockouts which would gravely imperil the public health, the public safety, or the general welfare. Two principal policies are possible. One is to give the government special emergency powers for dealing with such strikes or lockouts. The other is to give employees in certain essential industries a special status which gives them special privileges but imposes on them the obligation to refrain from striking. Let us compare these two possibilities.

When the public health, public safety, or general welfare is imperiled by a strike or a threat of strike, the government, of course, must do the best it can to protect the public interest. The government may call the parties into conference and plead with them to compromise or to submit their differences to arbitration. In the case of the railroads, the government may delay the crisis by appointing an emergency board. The government may warn the parties of the wrath of the public and may threaten them with adverse legislation.

It is not fair to public officers or to the community that the government be limited merely to pleading and threatening. If a threatened or actual strike or lockout seriously limits or threatens to limit the output of essential goods, the President (or in the case of states, the governor) should have the duty to declare that a state of emergency exists. Such a declaration should require the union to rescind any strike instructions and to order back to work any members who may have struck. In the case of a lockout, the declaration of public emergency should require that employers continue operations.

Union members who failed to obey the return-to-work order should be disciplined by the union in accordance with its laws in the same way that the union ordinarily disciplines the members who violate its rules. Failure of men to return to work, in addition, should terminate their employment. This would mean that they would be rehired by their employer as new employees with the seniority rights, vacation rights, and pension rights of new employees. In order to prevent the men from bargaining over the restoration of their rights, it should be made an unfair labor practice for employers to rehire them except as new employees. Picketing in support of strikes which have been found to imperil the public health, public safety, or general welfare should be forbidden and also the payment of strike benefits and other activities designed to promote illegal shutdowns. The union which failed to order its members back to work or which failed to discipline the members who violated its orders should be required by the National Labor Relations Board to show cause why it should not be deprived of its bargaining rights in the affected plants until such time as it showed that it had become a responsible organization.

The parties should be given three options for settling the dispute. They might agree to resume negotiations or they might submit the dispute to arbitrators selected by themselves. If they were unwilling or unable to use either of these two procedures, the dispute should be submitted to arbitrators selected by some independent agency. The head of the Conciliation Service would be an appropriate person to select arbitrators in case the parties fail to select them. The findings of the board should be retroactive to the expiration date of the previous contract, but should not be binding very far into the future. Six months is a reasonable period; it is short enough not to be onerous to either party, and it is long enough to give the parties an opportunity to negotiate a lasting settlement of their own.

The proposed policy restricts as little as possible the right to strike. It is flexible because it gives public officials a chance to use their own judgment about declaring an emergency. Particularly important is the fact that the policy works through unions and gives them the opportunity for becoming instruments to protect the community against disastrous interruptions to service.

Some people may object to the policy of giving emergency powers to the government for dealing with strikes in essential industries on the ground that it does not squarely face realities. In electric light and power, railroading, and a few other essential industries, the public cannot permit the parties to see which can stand the longer shutdown. All of this means that the men in essential industries, such as electric light and power and railroads, do not really have the right to strike; they have the right *only so long as they do not use it,* except on a very limited scale.

Is it not unfair to both the men and the public to pretend that the men have rights which the public will not tolerate their using? Is not the honest and fair procedure for the community to give "special status" to

the holders of jobs on which public health, public safety, and general welfare require continuous service?
Workers who accept employment on these jobs should
undertake not to engage in strikes. No union should be
eligible to bargain for workers on these jobs unless its
constitution prohibits strikes by members who hold
these jobs.

It is important, however, that the holders of "special
status" jobs be given special privileges as well as special
duties. In other words, it is important that they regard
themselves as fortunate in having especially desirable
jobs, jobs which they would not care to jeopardize by
going on strike. Hence, workers on special status jobs
should be assured that their wages will be reviewed
once a year and increased as rapidly as wages in general
rise. In addition, the special status workers should receive more liberal vacation privileges than employees
in general and more liberal pensions than those provided in the Social Security Act. The railway employees, of course, already receive larger pensions than
the Social Security Act provides.

Which of these two policies for protecting itself
against strikes in essential industries should a community adopt? The policy which is preferable is the
one which commands more complete and understanding support from the community. Especially in the field
of labor laws is it imperative that legislation reflect the
understanding of problems by the man-in-the-street.
Otherwise he will be unprepared to give legislation
the support which it must have in order to work satisfactorily.

Undoubtedly the sounder policy would be for the community to decide whether or not it can tolerate strikes in given occupations and, if it decides that it cannot, to provide special arrangements to assure that the employees will not suffer because they lack the right to strike. The man-in-the-street may not yet be prepared to do this. Millions of Americans, however, have observed the government's use of makeshift and possibly illegal instruments in its attempts to deal with strikes which created great public emergencies. They realize that the government must not again be left so helpless. Hence, the man-in-the-street is undoubtedly prepared to give the government emergency powers. He may not yet be prepared, however, to give employees in certain essential industries a special status which would compensate them for the fact that even today they do not really have the right to strike.

VI

What can be done to realize the tremendous potentialities of unions for good? What are these potentialities? They are many, but three are of particular importance:

1. That unions will help build a friendlier and more cooperative community in which different economic groups know more about each other's problems, take a greater interest in each other's problems, and have a greater capacity to work together.

2. That, as a result of the more effective representation of the interests of employees, the policies of industry will better reflect the needs of various groups in the community.

3. That, as a result of more adequate knowledge by various

groups of the problems of other groups and as a result of business policies which more effectively take account of the needs of workers, co-operation between employees and management in production will be more readily achieved and output per man-hour will be greater.

These are important possibilities for good. If the trade union movement can help materially to achieve them, it will be making an important contribution toward building a great civilization in America. Two great dangers exist. One is that trade unions will choose to be, in the main, militant rather than co-operative organizations. Many an organization today seeks to hold and to gain members by fostering fear, suspicion, and hatred of employers and by representing itself to prospective members as an organization which drives a good bargain for its members because it is tough. Few greater calamities could befall the community, including the workers themselves, than for the trade union movement to adopt a policy of militancy rather than one of co-operation with employers. It would mean, of course, that trade unions would be an agency for maintaining a wide gulf between managements and employees and for preventing workers from becoming interested in the problems of management and management from being interested in the problems of workers. It would mean that effective co-operation between employers and unions in pursuit of common interests (such as more production) would be seriously limited.

A second great danger is that trade unions will be parochial in their outlook, that each union will encourage its members to take a narrow view of their interests, to think of themselves primarily as bricklayers, steel workers, coal miners, or locomotive engineers, rather than as members of the community, and to attach less importance than they otherwise would to interests which they have in common with other economic groups. Such a development would also be a major calamity. The capacity of groups to co-operate depends upon their scales of value. If people are narrow and parochial, if they think mainly of their own occupational interests, the level of public spirit drops and the community becomes less able to deal effectively with community-wide problems and to formulate policies which are truly national.

Trade unions, of course, are not the only organizations which threaten to induce the members of the community to accept scales of value in which special interests rank too high in relation to interests which all groups have in common. This is an age of organization — of large business concerns and of innumerable associations of manufacturers, farmers, wholesalers, retailers. More and more, men's thinking and actions are determined by the policy decisions of these organizations. The interests which are most important, however, are the interests which are common to *all* groups in the community — for example, the maintenance of a high and steady level of employment and of a healthy rate of expansion, the preservation of a reasonably high business birth rate, and of a good opportunity for men and capital to enter new industries. Hence the spread of group organization must not be permitted to cause men to become so absorbed in the pursuit of particular interests that they neglect the more important common interests.

What can be done to induce the trade union movement, on the whole, to pursue co-operative rather than militant policies and to prevent trade unions from becoming narrow and parochial? Greater knowledge of the economics of wages and of the possibilities and limitations of collective bargaining would promote co-operative rather than militant policies, because such knowledge would help to prevent both employers and unions from expecting too much from collective bargaining. The need of such knowledge and its effect upon negotiations were discussed in Chapter III.

A great responsibility for the basic nature of union policies rests upon employers because the policies which employers pursue toward unions are a major determinant of the policies which unions pursue toward employers. Some unions and some union leaders, of course, have such fixed and unalterable objectives and methods that no change in policy on the part of employers would have much effect upon the behavior of the union. Nevertheless, as a general rule, the employer who seeks to build up goodwill and co-operation by treating the union with consideration and by showing a sincere interest in its problems will arouse a reciprocal spirit of goodwill in the union representatives and reciprocal interest in the problems of his business. In Chapter II some specific steps were outlined by which employers might build up a better day-to-day relationship with unions. In Chapter V suggestions were offered for improving negotiating procedure. More important than any specific procedures, however, is the spirit in which the management deals with the union. It is more desirable that union leaders sense a spirit of friendship and goodwill and a general interest in their problems than that the employer pursue methods of administration and negotiation which are correct by technical standards.

In large part, the responsibility of helping the trade union movement to develop co-operative rather than militant policies and to become an instrument for interesting workers in the broad problems of the community rather than for making workers narrow and parochial rests upon the community itself. It is important that the community be quick to assert the interests of the general public and that it impose high standards of behavior upon both employers and unions. Some of these standards have already been suggested. For example, the community should have a way of challenging make-work rules or restrictions on technological changes which are introduced into trade agreements. It should develop criteria for fair wage adjustments, for a good negotiating procedure, for good trade agreements. It should expect trade unions and employers to meet certain high standards in conducting negotiations and it should require them to show good cause for refusing to submit their deadlocks to arbitration. It should limit the use of strikes and boycotts for certain purposes, such as to compel employers to violate the law. It should also limit the use of strikes and lockouts in certain essential industries, such as electric light and

power and railroads. All of these standards and restraints, whether implemented by the moral force of
public opinion or by legal sanctions, would limit the
attractiveness of aggressive and militant policies by
employers and trade unions and thus would improve
the chance that each side would adopt co-operative
policies. Furthermore, since the standards and restraints impel unions and employers to think in terms
of the interests of the community, they tend to broaden
the viewpoint of union members and employers and to
counteract any tendency for unions or employers to
adhere to narrow and parochial policies.

Finally, a shift of power and influence from the
national unions to the two great federations — the
American Federation of Labor and the Congress of
Industrial Organizations — would help the trade union
movement develop co-operation with employers and
would help prevent the national unions from making
their members unduly limited in outlook. The interests
of labor as a whole, as I have pointed out several times,
diverge less seriously from interests of employers than
do the interests of the workers in a particular occupation or industry. Hence one may expect the federations to stand for more co-operative policies and to
take a less parochial view of labor's interests than do
the national unions.

A shift in power and influence from the national
unions to the two great federations would undoubtedly
be in the interest of labor itself. The mere fact that
employees are well organized to advance their interests
in particular crafts and industries but weakly organized

to advance the interests of labor as a whole means that the general interests of labor receive inadequate representation.

What are the chances that the federations will gain in power and influence in the labor movement? One hardly dares be optimistic. The principle of autonomy upon which the American labor movement has been based is still strong. One detects no signs within the trade unions themselves that the power and influence of the two federations will be increased. The division in the labor movement between the American Federation of Labor and the Congress of Industrial Organizations tends to increase the power of the nationals and to diminish the power of the federations. Undoubtedly American trade unionists will sooner or later awake to the fact that the interests of labor as a whole must in general take precedence over the interests of small groups of workers and that the organization of the labor movement must reflect this fact. The professional labor leaders, who are so important in the trade union movement of this country, are nearly all identified with particular national unions. Hence, few of them would care to see the federations gain greater power and influence at the expense of the nationals. One is forced to the conclusions (1) that the American trade union movement badly needs a shift of power and influence from national unions to the two federations, and (2) that such a shift of power and influence is not likely to occur in the foreseeable future. Let us hope that this forecast is wrong.

VII

The community will not find it easy to master the multitude of problems which have been created by the spectacular rise of trade unions and the great power which they have suddenly acquired. It is inevitable that such a rapid change will outrun the thinking of the community. I have pointed out several times how profoundly unprepared the country is to cope with these new problems — both intellectually unprepared and emotionally unprepared. This is not surprising. The present difficulties, however, are in the main temporary. The community will gradually learn the new facts and master the new problems which have been so suddenly thrust upon it.

Although the difficulties which confront the community are formidable, the reward for overcoming these difficulties is enormous. The organization of millions of workers into trade unions can tremendously improve the opportunities of workers to learn about the problems of employers and of employers to learn about the problems of workers. It gives employees powerful instruments for co-operating with other groups. It is true that these instruments may be used for fighting rather than for co-operating. If the potentialities for good in the trade union movement can be realized, however, America will build a civilization which surpasses all others in the capacity of the people to work together effectively in the pursuit of common aims. A clear vision of the ways in which the organization of workers can make the community become more co-operative and better able to solve its problems should spur all employers and employees to make these potentialities become realities.

The Messenger Lectures

THIS BOOK in its original form consisted of six lectures which the author delivered at Cornell University in the fall term of 1946, namely, the Messenger Lectures on the Evolution of Civilization. That series was founded and its title was prescribed by Hiram J. Messenger, B.Litt., Ph.D., of Hartford, Connecticut, who directed in his will that a portion of his estate be given to Cornell University and used to provide annually "a course or courses of lectures on the evolution of civilization, for the special purpose of raising the moral standard of our political, business, and social life." The lectureship was established in 1923.

Appendix A

APPROVAL OF STRIKE ACTION
AS REVEALED BY UNION CONSTITUTIONS

The following fifty-three A. F. of L. unions require national approval of strikes before they are legal under the union laws:

Automobile Workers
Bakery and Confectionery Workers
Blacksmiths, Drop Forgers and Helpers
Boilermakers, Iron Shipbuilders and Helpers
Bookbinders
Brick and Clay Workers
Bricklayers, Masons and Plasterers
Bridge and Structural Iron Workers
Building Service Employees
Broom and Whisk Makers
Carpenters and Joiners
Cement, Lime and Gypsum Workers
Cigar Makers
Cleaning and Dye House Workers
Diamond Workers
Electrical Workers, Brotherhood of
Elevator Constructors
Fire Fighters
Firemen and Oilers

Flint Glass Workers
Garment Workers, United
Glass Bottle Blowers
Granite Cutters
Hatters, Cap and Millinery Workers
Horse Shoers
Lathers
Laundry Workers
Leather Workers
Longshoremen
Maintenance of Way Employees
Metal Polishers, Buffers, Platers and Helpers
Molders and Foundry Workers
Painters, Decorators and Paperhangers
Paper Makers
Pattern Makers
Photo-Engravers
Potters
Printing Pressmen
Pulp, Sulphite and Paper Mill Workers
Railway and Steamship Clerks

Shoe Workers
Stage Employees and Moving
  Picture Machine Operators
Stereotypers & Electrotypers
Stonecutters
Stove Mounters
Street, Electric Railway and
  Motor Coach Employees
Switchmen

Teamsters, Chauffeurs, Ware-
  housemen and Helpers
Telegraphers, Commercial
Tobacco Workers
Typographical Union
Upholsterers
Wall Paper Craftsmen and
  Workers

The following six A. F. of L. unions require approval by the national in nearly all cases but permit locals to call strikes without national approval in some cases:

Coopers
Garment Workers, Ladies'
Meat Cutters and Butcher
  Workmen

Musicians
Plumbers and Steam Fitters
Mine Workers

The following twenty-four C.I.O. national unions require national approval of strikes before they are legal under the union laws:

Automobile, Aircraft and Im-
  plement Workers
Barbers and Beauty
  Culturists
Electrical, Radio and
  Machine Workers
Farm Equipment and Metal
  Workers
Food, Tobacco, Agricultural
  and Allied Workers
Fur and Leather Workers
Gas, Coke and Chemical
  Workers
Glass, Ceramic, and Silica
  Sand Workers
Marine and Shipbuilders
Marine Engineers
Maritime Union

Mine, Mill, and Smelter
  Workers
Oil Workers
Packinghouse Workers
Playthings and Novelty
  Workers
Public Workers, United
Retail, Wholesale, and
  Department Store
  Employees
Rubber, Cork, Linoleum, and
  Plastic Workers
Shoe Workers
Steelworkers
Stone and Allied Product
  Workers
Textile Workers
Transport Service Employees
Transport Workers' Union

The following three C.I.O. unions require approval by the national in nearly all cases:

Brewery, Flour, Cereal and
    Soft Drink Workers
Lithographers

Office and Professional
    Workers of America

Appendix B

APPOINTMENT OF INTERNATIONAL
REPRESENTATIVES

In the following thirty-six A. F. of L. national unions, the appointment of international representatives is the exclusive responsibility of the president:

Automobile Workers
Barbers and Hairdressers
Boilermakers, Iron Ship-
    builders and Helpers
Boot and Shoe Workers
Brick and Clay Workers
Bridge and Structural Iron
    Workers
Carpenters and Joiners
Cleaning and Dye House
    Workers
Coopers
Electrical Workers,
    Brotherhood of
Elevator Constructors
Engineers, Operating
Firemen and Oilers

Hod Carriers
Horse Shoers
Hotel and Restaurant
    Employees
Jewelry Workers
Longshoremen
Maintenance of Way
    Employees
Masters, Mates and Pilots
Meat Cutters and Butcher
    Workmen[1]
Metal Polishers, Buffers,
    Platers and Helpers
Musicians
Painters, Decorators and
    Paperhangers
Post Office Clerks

---

[1] Organizers are appointed jointly by the president and the secretary-treasurer.

Postal Supervisors
Printing Pressmen
Railroad Telegraphers
Railway Carmen
Stage Employees and Moving
    Picture Machine Operators

Street, Electric Railway and
    Motor Coach Employees
Switchmen
Telegraphers, Commercial
Tobacco Workers
Typographical Union
Upholsterers

In the following twenty A. F. of L. unions, international representatives are appointed by the president with the approval of the executive board:

Asbestos Workers
Blacksmiths, Drop Forgers
    and Helpers
Bookbinders
Building Service Employees
Cement, Lime and Gypsum
    Workers
Cigar Makers
Government Employees
Garment Workers, Ladies'
Handbag, Luggage, Belt and
    Novelty Workers

Hatters, Cap and Millinery
    Workers
Laundry Workers
Mine Workers
Molders & Foundry Workers
Paper Makers
Photo-Engravers
Plasterers
Pulp, Sulphite and Paper
    Mill Workers
Retail Clerks
Textile Workers
Stereotypers & Electrotypers

In the following three A. F. of L. unions, international representatives are appointed by the executive board:

Bakery Workers   Granite Cutters   Teachers

In the following C.I.O. union, the appointment of international representatives is the exclusive responsibility of the president:

Clothing Workers, Amalgamated

In the following twenty-one C.I.O. unions, international representatives are appointed by the president with the approval of the executive board:

Automobile, Aircraft and
    Implement Workers
Communications Association

Farm Equipment and Metal
    Workers
Fishermen

Food, Tobacco, Agricultural and Allied Workers
Furniture Workers
Gas, Coke and Chemical Workers
Glass, Ceramic and Silica Sand Workers
Lithographers
Marine and Shipbuilders
Mine, Mill and Smelter Workers
Office and Professional Workers
Oil Workers
Public Workers, United
Retail, Wholesale and Department Store Employees
Rubber Workers
Shoe Workers
Steelworkers
Textile Workers
Transport Service Employees
Transport Workers' Union

In the following five C.I.O. unions, international representatives are appointed by the executive board:

Barbers and Beauty Culturists
Brewery Workers
Electrical Workers
Fur Workers
Packinghouse Workers

Appendix C

PRESIDENTIAL POWERS LIMITED BY EXECUTIVE BOARD

In the following twenty A. F. of L. unions, the president may appoint international officers with the approval of the executive board:

Asbestos Workers
Blacksmiths
Bookbinders
Building Service Employees
Cement, Lime and Gypsum Workers
Cigar Makers
Government Employees
Garment Workers, Ladies'
Handbag, Luggage, Belt and Novelty Workers

Hatters, Cap and Millinery Workers
Laundry Workers
Mine Workers
Molders and Foundry Workers
Paper Makers

Photo-Engravers
Plasterers
Pulp, Sulphite and Paper Mill Workers
Retail Clerks
Textile Workers
Stereotypers & Electrotypers

In the following twelve A. F. of L. unions, the president may remove representatives with the approval of the board:

Bookbinders
Carpenters and Joiners
Elevator Constructors
Jewelry Workers
Mine Workers
Paper Makers

Photo-Engravers
Railway Mail Association
Retail Clerks
Stereotypers
Stone Cutters
Upholsterers

In the following twenty A. F. of L. unions, the president may suspend or revoke local charters with the approval of the board:

Blacksmiths, Drop Forgers and Helpers
Boilermakers, Iron Shipbuilders and Helpers
Boot and Shoe Workers
Carpenters and Joiners
Cleaning and Dye House Workers
Hotel and Restaurant Employees
Laundry Workers
Longshoremen
Mine Workers

Molders and Foundry Workers
Potters
Railroad Telegraphers
Railway Carmen
Railway and Steamship Clerks
Stone Cutters
Street, Electric Railway and Motor Coach Employees
Teamsters
Telegraphers, Commercial
Textile Workers
Upholsterers

APPENDIXES

In the following twenty-seven A. F. of L. unions, the president may discipline or supplant local officers with the approval of the board:

Asbestos Workers
Automobile Workers
Blacksmiths
Boilermakers, Iron Ship-
   builders and Helpers
Bookbinders
Building Service Employees
Cement, Lime and Gypsum
   Workers
Cleaning and Dye House
   Workers
Elevator Constructors
Garment Workers, Ladies'
Glass Cutters, Window
Hatters, Cap and Millinery
   Workers
Hod Carriers
Hotel and Restaurant
   Employees
Mine Workers
Molders and Foundry
   Workers
Painters, Decorators and
   Paperhangers
Paper Makers
Railroad Telegraphers
Railway Carmen
Railway Mail Association
Railway and Steamship
   Clerks
Retail Clerks
Stage Employees and Moving
   Picture Machine Operators
Telegraphers, Commercial
Upholsterers
Wall Paper Craftsmen and
   Workers

In the following twenty-one C.I.O. unions, the president may appoint international officers with the approval of the executive board:

Automobile, Aircraft and
   Implement Workers
Communications Association
Farm Equipment and Metal
   Workers
Fishermen
Food, Tobacco, Agricultural
   and Allied Workers
Furniture Workers
Gas, Coke and Chemical
   Workers
Glass, Ceramic and Silica
   Sand Workers
Lithographers
Marine and Shipbuilders
Mine, Mill and Smelter
   Workers
Office and Professional
   Workers
Oil Workers
Public Workers, United
Retail, Wholesale and
   Department Store
   Employees
Rubber Workers
Shoe Workers

Steelworkers

Textile Workers

Transport Service Employees

Transport Workers

In the following three C.I.O. unions, the president may suspend or revoke local charters with the approval of the board:

Farm Equipment and Metal
  Workers

Mine, Mill and Smelter
  Workers

Public Workers, United

In the following four C.I.O. unions, the president may discipline or supplant local officers with the approval of the board:

Farm Equipment and Metal
  Workers

Longshoremen and
  Warehousemen

Oil Workers

Rubber Workers

Appendix D

POWERS OF THE PRESIDENTS

In the following eight A. F. of L. unions, the president may remove any international officer and there is no appeal from his decision:

Bridge and Structural Iron
  Workers

Electrical Workers,
  Brotherhood of

Maintenance of Way
  Employees

Plumbers and Steamfitters[2]

Pulp, Sulphite and Paper
  Mill Workers

Street, Electric Railway and
  Motor Coach
  Employees[3]

Switchmen

Typographical Union

---

[2] The president is empowered to remove executive board members, all of whom are international officers. Impeachment must be by the executive board, at the instigation of a local.

[3] The president's power is limited to suspension. Expulsion must be by the executive board, subject to appeal to the convention.

APPENDIXES

In the following thirteen A. F. of L. unions, the president may suspend and revoke charters of locals without appeal:

Bridge and Structural Iron
  Workers
Electrical Workers,
  Brotherhood of
Engineers, Operating
Glass Bottle Blowers
Leather Workers
Maintenance of Way
  Employees
Musicians

Painters, Decorators and
  Paperhangers
Paper Makers
Plumbers and Steamfitters
Pulp, Sulphite and Paper
  Mill Workers
Stage Employees and Moving
  Picture Machine Operators
Switchmen

In the following twelve A. F. of L. unions, the president may discipline and replace local officers without appeal:

Bricklayers, Masons and
  Plasterers[4]
Bridge and Structural Iron
  Workers
Engineers, Operating
Electrical Workers,
  Brotherhood of
Glass Bottle Blowers

Lathers
Meat Cutters and Butcher
  Workmen
Musicians
Sleeping Car Porters
Switchmen
Teamsters
Typographical Workers

In the following three C.I.O. unions, the president has the power to discipline or supplant local officers without appeal:

Glass, Ceramic and Silica Workers
Mine, Mill and Smelter Workers
Office and Professional Workers

---

[4] The executive board suspends local members. The president has power to appoint a person to administer the affairs of a local union.

Appendix E

POWERS OF EXECUTIVE BOARDS

In the following fifteen A. F. of L. unions, the executive board may remove an international officer without appeal:

Asbestos Workers
Barbers and Hairdressers
Boot and Shoe Workers
Bricklayers, Masons and
  Plasterers
Broom and Whisk Makers
Fire Fighters
Garment Workers, Ladies'
Garment Workers, United

Glass Cutters, Window
Handbag, Luggage, Belt and
  Novelty Workers
Hod Carriers
Lathers
Leather Workers
Letter Carriers
Molders and Foundry
  Workers

In the following twenty-five A. F. of L. unions, the executive board may suspend or revoke local charters:

Asbestos Workers
Automobile Workers
Bakery and Confectionery
  Workers
Barbers and Hairdressers
Bricklayers
Broom and Whisk Makers[5]
Building Service Employees
Coopers
Garment Workers, Ladies'
Garment Workers, United
Government Employees
Granite Workers

Handbag, Luggage, Belt
  and Novelty Workers
Hatters, Cap and Millinery
  Workers
Hod Carriers
Jewelry Workers[6]
Masters, Mates and Pilots
Meat Cutters
Metal Polishers, Buffers,
  Platers and Helpers
Mine, Mill and Smelter
  Workers

---

[5] The president, with the consent of the executive board and subject to appeal to the membership, has power to suspend a charter. Revocation of a charter is a power of the executive board.

[6] The president, with the consent of the executive board, has the power to suspend charters. Revocation of a charter is a power of the executive board.

[188]

APPENDIXES

Railway Mail Association
Retail Clerks
Stereotypers & Electrotypers

Typographical Union
Wall Paper Craftsmen
and Workers

In the following eleven A. F. of L. unions, the executive board may discipline and supplant local officers:

Diamond Workers
Garment Workers, United
Glove Workers
Government Employees
Handbag, Luggage, Belt and
Novelty Workers

Horse Shoers
Metal Polishers
Plasterers
Printing Pressmen
Textile Workers
Tobacco Workers

In the following six C.I.O. unions, the executive board may remove an international officer without appeal:

Automobile, Aircraft and
Implement Workers
Inland Boatmen's Union
Marine and Shipbuilders'
Union

Office and Professional
Workers
Steelworkers
Transport Workers' Union

In the following twelve C.I.O. unions, the executive board may suspend or revoke local charters:

Automobile, Aircraft and
Implement Workers
Barbers and Beauty
Culturists
Gas, Coke and Chemical
Workers
Newspaper Guild
Office and Professional
Workers

Oil Workers
Retail, Wholesale and
Department Store
Employees
Rubber Workers
Shoe Workers
Textile Workers
Transport Service Employees
Transport Workers' Union

In the following seven C.I.O. unions, the executive board may discipline and supplant local officers:

Automobile, Aircraft and
Implement Workers
Fishermen
Inland Boatmen's Union
Newspaper Guild

Playthings and Novelty
Workers
Retail, Wholesale and
Department Store
Employees
Transport Workers' Union

Index

INDEX

INDEX

Men and boys' clothing industry, 76–77
Metal trades, 145
Militancy, policy of, 171–175
Monopolistic competition, 30–31
Morse, Senator Wayne, 68
Motion picture operators, 103
Musicians' union, 114

National income, share of union members in, 91–95
National Industrial Recovery Act, 11
National Labor Relations Board, 55, 68, 119, 120, 157, 160, 167
National net product, 19, 32, 73, 74
National officers, *see* Union officers, national
National unions,
    administration of agreements by, 106
    admission policies of, 103
    control of funds by, 105
    control of strikes by, 105–106
    development of, 6, 7–8
    number of, 3, 16
    policy-executing in, 105–107
    policy-making in, 103–105
    problems arising from, 8
Naumkeag Steam Spinning Company, 40–41
Negotiations, methods of, 24, 106, 126, 129, 130, 131–138, 138–145, 152–153, 167, 174
Negroes, 102–103, 118
Nonunion labor, substituted for union labor, 92, 93, 94
Nonunion shops, layoffs in, 34
Norris-LaGuardia Act, 11

Offenses, vague, 110–111, 116
Officers, union, *see* Union officers
Older workers, 34
Oligopoly, 31
Output, union limits upon, 44–45, 52, 59
Overtime work, 45

Padway, Joseph, 158, 159
Pension plans, 34, 55–56, 115–116
Pension rights, 163–164, 167, 169

Photo-engravers, 104
Picketing, 164, 167
Piece rates, setting of, 42
Policy-executing in unions, 9, 105–107, 116–118, 121
Policy-making in unions, 9, 103–105, 111–112, 116–118, 121
Political conditions in unions, 134–135
Postal Telegraph Company, 41
Presidents, union,
    powers of, 107–110
    tenure of office of, 113–114
Pressmen's union, 113
Prices,
    as affected by business cycle, 79–82
    as affected by rise in wages, 77–82
"Product-mix," 73, 91
Productivity, as basis for wage demands, 137
Profits,
    and saving, 83, 84
    and spending, 87
Promotion of workers, 37–38, 59, 62
Propensity to save, 83, 84
Public interest, trade unions and, 118–119, 123, Chapter VI: 154–178
Public policy,
    strikes to change, 26
    toward unions, 10, 11
    workers' stake in, 17

Rank and file, union, 15, 23, 40–41, 112, 117–118, 121, 134–135
Re-employment, after illegal strike, 164, 167
Representatives, union,
    as source of information, 56
    national, 107, 133
    relations with management, 62, 63
Retail Clerks' International Protective Association, 109
Right to strike, *see* Strikes, right of
Rivalries, between labor leaders and between unions, *see* Competition
Robinson, Mrs. Joan, 78n

Savings function, 79n, 84, 85
Seidman, Joel, 102n, 109n

[193]

INDEX